Thomas Middleton's
City Comedies

Thomas Middleton's City Comedies

Anthony Covatta

Lewisburg
Bucknell University Press

© 1973 by Associated University Presses, Inc.

Associated University Presses, Inc.
Cranbury, New Jersey 08512

Library of Congress Cataloging in Publication Data

Covatta, Anthony, 1944–
    Thomas Middleton's city comedies.

    Bibliography: p.
    1. Middleton, Thomas, d. 1627. I. Title.
PR2717.C6 1973   822'.3   72-3261
ISBN 0-8387-1196-0

For Neil

Contents

Preface

I first encountered Middleton's City Comedies several summers ago, while studying for my doctoral orals. Despite that impending melancholy appointment, the time was pleasant indeed, especially when an afternoon's reading included *A Mad World, My Masters, Michaelmas Term,* or another of the comedies. I found the plays uproariously funny then; they are hardly less amusing to me now. Rereading my favorite passages still makes me laugh, and with deep appreciation. These plays are not "merely" humorous; quite often they are comedy at its best, forming an oblique but telling commentary on human experience, on its disconcerting, simultaneous tendency to chaos and to bewildering yet ordered complexity.

Middletonian criticism has not been so good as its subject. Much of it has been preoccupied with peripheral problems, considerations that even preclude a fair reading of the plays. Few critics see in Middleton the lightness and gaiety that Una Ellis-Fermor recognizes as integral to his art. In the last few years a new picture of the plays has begun to emerge, chiefly in articles and introductions by scholars such as Richard Levin, Standish Henning, Brian Parker, Arthur

F. Marotti, and Robert I. Williams. They have begun to introduce the notion of irony into the Middletonian critical vocabulary, to readjust the idea of Middleton as realist, to see the works as more complex, light-hearted creations than they have been thought. But no one has yet dealt with the City Comedies of Middleton exclusively and as a body, and treated them simply as works of art.

This I have tried to do, keeping in mind always that they are marvelous comic creations. I have focused only on Middleton, excluding collaborative efforts such as *The Roaring Girl,* in my opinion a much overrated play. Chronology has not been a major concern; determining when Middleton wrote what still seems a hopeless task. We simply do not have enough information to fix the canon. If the order of my treatment of the plays suggests a chronology, it offers no claim to proof and is meant only to be suggestive. I have found it necessary, though, to look closely at several of the basic premises of Middletonian comedy criticism before engaging the plays themselves. The notions of Middleton as realist, satirist, didacticist, reporter of socioeconomic tendencies, all need readjustment; a broader, more sympathetic base must be prepared before the dramas can be viewed to best advantage.

My study of the economic and social background, of the writing habits of the Jacobeans, of the nature of comedy, satire, and irony convinced me that these plays should be studied not as social documents but as fictions. They can best be seen as dramatic constructs, put together by a man of considerable intelligence, wit, and dramatic skill. They are as excellent, as funny as they are, precisely because they are very literary works, derived from and part of an age-old tradition of stock forms, characters, and situations.

Middleton did not just borrow. He added much to the materials he inherited. Over a period of time he learned to structure character, incident, form, and theme in patterns no less complicated than humorous. Through much of that period his work is marred by a curious dualism, a tendency to accept and reject the world simultaneously. However, his major comedies are far more positive than negative about their subject matter. We can see that, in his best work, Middleton stands the world on its head and enjoys doing so, portraying a vision in which the last are always first and the first last. Values are inverted, expectations reversed, all balanced in a breathtaking display of symmetry. In his carefully planned, skillfully wrought chaos, we can appreciate at once something of life's absurdity and value, and over a considerable range of human experience.

It comes time now to thank those humans who lessened life's absurdity for me, whose acquaintance I value. S. F. Johnson sponsored an earlier version of this book as my dissertation at Columbia; he was a wise and discreet mentor. Daniel Dodson was more than helpful as teacher and boss. Had George Stade and John Unterecker not extended kindnesses to me in my student days, I might not have been in a position to write this book at all. David George took time from a busy schedule at the Folger Library to share his knowledge of Middleton with me; I am grateful for his generosity. The Skidmore Faculty Research Committee awarded me two grants toward completion of the work, which I gratefully acknowledge. Colleagues at Skidmore, Ralph Ciancio, Patricia-Ann Lee, and Patrick Keane, read portions of the manuscript; I profited from their counsel. Mrs. Betsy Delay was a good-humored, patient, and sure-fingered typist. The dedication acknowledges my greatest debt; happily, it can never be fully paid.

Saratoga Springs, New York

Acknowledgments

Excerpts from Thomas Middleton's *Michaelmas Term,* ed. Richard Levin, reprinted by permission of University of Nebraska Press. Copyright © 1966 by the University of Nebraska Press. Excerpts from Thomas Middleton's *A Mad World, My Masters,* ed. Standish Henning, reprinted by permission of University of Nebraska Press. Copyright © 1965 by the University of Nebraska Press. Quotations from *A Chaste Maid in Cheapside* are drawn from the Revels Plays Edition of R. B. Parker (London, 1969). All other citations are from the standard edition of Middleton's works in eight volumes, ed. A. H. Bullen (London, 1885-86), hereafter referred to as *Works.*

An earlier version of chapter 3, called "Coming of Age in *Michaelmas Term,*" was read to a section of the April 1972 convention of the Northeastern Modern Language Association. My thanks to Richard Morton, the section head, and all those who received the paper so graciously.

Thomas Middleton's
City Comedies

1

The Issues

THOMAS Middleton was a prolific writer, the author, in whole or in part, of about 25 plays; but he was relatively neglected in his own time and has received a respectable amount of attention only in our century. We are just now beginning to have a body of Middleton criticism, although the bulk has not become overwhelming. Four book-length studies, varied in format and value, have been published in the last fifty years. The essays and sections devoted to the playwright in larger studies make up a modest list, far shorter than Ben Jonson's.[1]

1. The books include W. D. Dunkel, *The Dramatic Technique of Thomas Middleton in His Comedies of London Life* (Chicago, 1925); Samuel Schoenbaum, *Middleton's Tragedies* (New York, 1955); Richard Hindry Barker, *Thomas Middleton* (New York, 1958); David Holmes, *The Art of Thomas Middleton* (Oxford, 1970). Dunkel deals only with the comedies, Schoenbaum the tragedies, Barker and Holmes with both. Dunkel's study is decidedly dated; though Barker's is quite general, it is often of some value and will be cited in the course of the work. Holmes's book will convince only those who already share its assumptions. Essays that take an overview are mentioned below; those dealing with specific plays will be cited at the appropriate places in the text. Two valuable general studies are: M. C. Bradbrook, *The Growth and Structure of Elizabethan Comedy* (London, 1955); Una Ellis-Fermor, *The Jacobean Drama,* 5th ed. (London, 1965).

This moderate amount of material presents a rather fragmentary critical picture. Perhaps Middleton has not been studied more thoroughly because he makes a forbidding subject. Biographical material is scanty.[2] Middleton seldom refers to himself in his writings, even indirectly; and the works themselves seem to reveal two playwrights, one with a tragic, one a comic sensibility. Some critics even seem to think him unworthy of study; Jonson's is the first recorded low opinion of Middleton, but hardly the last.[3] Middleton's facility at writing in many different genres and styles, often with more competence than distinction, has also caused a number of later commentators to discount him. But even if we admit that he could perform at very low artistic levels, a cursory survey of the criticism we do possess will show that he can be taken seriously, although there is some controversy over just where his value lies.

I

T. S. Eliot's 1927 essay is still one of the most important pieces on Middleton.[4] Eliot attempts to be sympathetic to the playwright, calling him one of the best dramatists of his age, the author of six or seven great plays. By allowing him such a large number of great works, Eliot unavoidably includes some of the comedies, although he does not discuss them at length. This short notice, more arithmetic than aesthetic, has done much to create interest in the plays. But Eliot's essay is not entirely positive. He finds obstacles to the study of Middleton. Unable to discern tone or texture recognizably "Middletonian," Eliot concedes the playwright

---

2. A short summary of Middleton's life is included in an appendix, along with a chronology of the plays. The fullest account of the life appears in Barker, pp. 1–25.

3. Ben Jonson, *Works*, ed. C. H. Herford, Percy and Evelyn Simpson (Oxford, 1925–52), 1:137. Jonson told Drummond of Hawthornden that Middleton was "a base fellow."

4. T. S. Eliot, "Thomas Middleton," *Selected Essays*, new ed. (New York, 1964), pp. 140–48.

neither personality nor point of view. He grants only that his name is a label that does associate some great plays. Although it seems strange to find the father of the objective correlative distressed at impersonality, the criticism has had its effect. Even today some tend to think Middleton impersonal and, in ethical terms, amoral, to say that his plays show no moral concern either in general design or in the portrayal of specific characters.

This consideration is older by some years than Eliot's essay. It seems to have arisen in the nineteenth century when late-Victorian critics generally praised Middleton's works, although they were shocked by the "gross material" used "grossly."[5]

Critics have long felt that Middleton found the rank subject matter for his plays in the London streets. Eliot cites Kathleen Lynch as his authority on the matter, but her remarks on Middleton's "thorough-going realism" and hearty observation of life at first hand[6] are not the only source for the doctrine of Middletonian realism. Earlier remarks, like Felix Schelling's that Middleton was "the most absolute realist in the Elizabethan drama" have lodged themselves just as firmly in critical memory.[7]

Eliot, however, was probably the first to articulate another critical commonplace: the great disparity between Middleton's best comedies and best tragedies, a problem that may account for Eliot's inability to see a man behind the plays. In recent years some have tried to find the coherence Eliot thought lacking.[8] R. B. Parker finds in Middle-

---

5. Thomas Middleton. *Works,* ed. Algernon Charles Swinburne (London, n.d.), pp. xxxvii–xxxviii. See also *Works,* 1: xcii *et passim;* A. W. Ward, *A History of English Dramatic Literature* (London, 1899), 2:521; CHEL 6, Part II (1910):71–74.

6. *The Social Mode of Restoration Comedy* (New York, 1926), p. 24.

7. Felix Schelling, *Elizabethan Drama* (Boston, 1908), 1:516.

8. See R. B. Parker, "Middleton's Experiments with Comedy and Judgement," *Jacobean Theatre,* ed. John Russell Brown and Bernard Harris (New York, 1960), pp. 179–200; Samuel Schoenbaum, "*A Chaste Maid in Cheapside* and Middleton's City Comedy," *Studies in English Renaissance Drama in Memory of Karl Julius Holzknecht,* ed. J. W. Bennett *et al.* (New York, 1959), pp. 287–309.

ton tension between skillful portrayal of manners and desire to denounce immorality. He asserts that Middleton found it difficult to condemn immoral characters severely. This caused an uneasiness of tone, a moral discomfort, which appears in all his early comedies, becomes clearer in *A Trick* and *Chaste Maid,* and evolves into the dark and bloody world of *Women, Beware Women.* Samuel Schoenbaum takes almost the same approach. For him *Chaste Maid* maintains a tension between the essential brutality of its material and the laughter informing the action. This last great comedy, the most somber of Middleton's works in the genre, points toward the later, even more somber tragedies. Though both studies are remarkable pieces of work, neither is entirely convincing. The disparity remains.

A man writes at different times, for different purposes. It is not so necessary to insist on a writer's unity of purpose as to take account of all his major impulses. Shakespeare wrote both *As You Like It* and *Titus Andronicus,* and it seems more profitable to understand each of them than to tie them tightly together. Most of Middleton's critics have obviated the difficulty of linking comedies and tragedies by limiting themselves to one of the two genres, as I will, to comedy. Until quite recently those who dealt with the comedies generally followed the lead of Eliot and his predecessors in considering Middleton realistic, impersonal, and even amoral, as they proceeded to investigate other aspects of his work. One of them, L. C. Knights, has probably been even more influential than Eliot.[9]

Knights's *Drama and Society in the Age of Jonson* is not solely responsible for the prevalence of the economic approach to Middleton, Jonson, Marston, and their lesser colleagues, but it is quite an important influence to that tendency.[10] Investigating the ways in which literature relates

9. *Drama and Society in the Age of Jonson* (London, 1937).
10. See Eliot, Lynch; K. L. Gregg, *Thomas Dekker: A Study in Economic and Social Backgrounds* (Seattle, 1924).

to society and social change, Knights asks whether cultural
activities are related to "bread-and-butter" activities such
as daily business pursuits and, if they are, what effect economic concerns have on them.[11] His argument will be detailed below; in summary he concludes that Middleton and
his colleagues relied on realistic techniques to mirror in their
plays the economic dislocation of the times. The playwright
distanced himself from his work and, as a special pleader,
lacked moral commitment.

Knights's treatise harmonizes well with Alfred Harbage's
theory of the organization of the Jacobean theater. Harbage
contends that there were two distinct theatrical traditions
in Jacobean England, at least until the time of Shakespeare's
retirement from active involvement in the King's Company.[12]
Shakespeare, Dekker, Heywood, and others worked in a
"popular" form while Middleton, Marston, Jonson, Chapman, and some lesser talents appealed to a "coterie" of
aristocratic patrons at more expensive, more exclusive
houses. This second group was composed largely of university men, uprooted by education from their social background.

The plays they wrote appealed to an equally dislocated
audience. The largely aristocratic coterie that was the main-
stay of the private houses delighted in works satirizing the
commercial classes. They could at least feel intellectually
and socially superior to those who were pushing them to the
wall economically. The writers, practical men as they had
to be, pitched their work to the predilections of their effete,
jaded clientele. According to Harbage, they had a weather
eye for social distinction, treating immoral gentlemen much
more kindly than immoral merchants. Social inferiority was

---

11. Knights, p. 3.
12. *Shakespeare and the Rival Traditions* (New York, 1952), p. 41; for
a recent study that views Middleton from a vantage point similar to Harbage's see Arthur C. Kirsch, *Jacobean Dramatic Perspectives* (Charlottesville, Va., 1972), pp. 75–96.

much more despised than moral inferiority.[13] Meanwhile the popular dramatists were thoroughly in tune with the nation at large, and with the ideals of liberal humanism. Godly, healthy, vigorous, chaste, the plays of Shakespeare and his colleagues were distinctly different from the lewd fare written for the private houses by Middleton and others.[14]

Harbage's tone makes one feel that he considers the works of Middleton, Marston, and the rest inferior creations, not worthy of mention, perhaps, next to the achievements of the popular dramatists. Few would proclaim any Jacobean Shakespeare's equal; but several plays from the private houses, including some of Middleton's, do possess considerable excellence. Richard Levin's recent work has demonstrated the elaborate artistry with which Middleton constructed his comedies.[15] He shows convincingly that there is nothing casual about these plays; they do not merely espouse one point of view. Instead, they are formed from a number of plots that counterpoint one another ethically and aesthetically. But Levin's studies are not so broad, balanced, and sympathetic as they might be. He holds some of Knights's and Harbage's basic premises, interpreting the chief action of the plays as class warfare following the economic revolution of the sixteenth century.[16] Consequently he treats the plays strictly as satires. In his view Middleton attacks both surface follies of London street life and the stupidities and evil inherent in a conflict between classes.

Brian Gibbons's recent study of City Comedy also is in-

---

13. Harbage, p. 77.
14. *Ibid.*, p. 221.
15. See his *The Multiple Plot in English Renaissance Drama* (Chicago, 1971), which incorporates his earlier studies: "The Dampit Scenes in *A Trick to Catch the Old One*," *MLQ* 25 (1964): 140–52; "The Four Plots of *A Chaste Maid in Cheapside*," *RES* 45 (1965): 14–24; "The Family of Lust and *The Family of Love*," *SEL* 6 (1966): 309–22.
16. As is reflected in the introduction to his edition of *Michaelmas Term*, Regents Renaissance Drama Series (Lincoln, Neb., 1966), p. xv. See *The Multiple Plot, passim.*

fluenced by Knights, though it claims to reconsider his premises.[17] But the work follows *Drama and Society* closely in format and point of view, even if it brings some new light to bear on the plays. For this critic too, Middleton's City Comedies, like Marston's and Jonson's, are wholly satiric.[18] Unfortunately, this approach forces Gibbons to neglect completely large portions of the action in each play. For him Middleton's plays are single actions centering around the vices and machinations of his old men. He insists, as his predecessors had, that the plays are constructed dialectically, and he invokes the notion of class struggle and civil war throughout his analysis. Gibbons's major advance is his attempt to modify the notion of Middleton's realism. He sees, quite correctly, that the plays are more schematic than representational; but he is hampered by his insistence on their didactic intent.

The latest book on Middleton insists on didactic intent to an extreme.[19] For David Holmes, Middleton was primarily a moralist, and a rather strict one. To reach this position Holmes must take Middleton's *juvenilia* far too seriously, ignore the nature and purpose of late Elizabethan verse satire, and then misinterpret the plays. For him, too, Middleton is a realistic observer of contemporary economic struggle. He goes so far as to compare the early Middleton to Zola, as Gibbons had compared him—and, even more, Jonson—to Brecht.[20]

Though the picture does not focus perfectly, in fact is somewhat confused, we can see that a number of notions dominate Middleton criticism, at least the major critiques of the comedies. Many tell us that he is a realist—a prevailing notion despite the efforts of some scholars to rethink

17. *Jacobean City Comedy* (Cambridge, Mass., 1968).
18. *Ibid.,* p. 24.
19. David M. Holmes, *The Art of Thomas Middleton* (Oxford, 1970).
20. *Ibid.,* p. 25; Gibbons, pp. 19–22.

the position.[21] There is also a feeling that he portrays the class struggle created by the economic and social dislocation of his times. Some say that he is impersonal, amoral, or even immoral; others that his plays are satiric, though few consider just what the term signifies. A few contend that Middleton is a fully committed moralist, a conscious didacticist.

Of course, contradictions are easy to come by in compilations of critical opinion. But these suppositions are open to further discussion even when they stand alone. A number of them are either incorrect or misleading. Several questions come to mind immediately. How can a satirist be amoral if satire presupposes some form of moral commitment? At the other extreme, would an audience seeking entertainment support works that are solely and overtly didactic? How does didactic drama show the balance necessary to art? This study will deal with these and other matters; with Middleton's attitude toward economic and social issues, his realism, his point of view, his literary morality. All these issues are, of course, subsumed under the larger question of the nature of Middleton's comedy. I will try to answer that after examining the issues in studying seven of Middleton's comedies: *A Chaste Maid in Cheapside* and the plays that led up to it, *The Family of Love, The Phoenix, Your Five Gallants, Michaelmas Term, A Trick to Catch the Old One,* and *A Mad World, My Masters.*[22] But first we must look at the world in which the plays are set.

---

21. In addition to Gibbons, see especially "Introduction," *A Mad World, My Masters,* ed. Standish Henning, Regents Renaissance Drama Series (Lincoln, Neb., 1965), pp. x–xvii; Robert I. Williams, "Machiavelli's *Mandragola,* Touchwood Senior, and the Comedy of Middleton's *A Chaste Maid in Cheapside,*" *SEL* 10 (1970) : 385–96. These two short studies contain some of the most sensible thinking on Middleton's supposed affinity for realistic techniques.

22. Plays written after *A Chaste Maid* are the products of other influences, and study of them involves different assumptions. There are a few other plays written in this period that are sometimes attributed to Middleton, but none of them seem centrally relevant to my argument, or necessary for its illustration.

II

L. C. Knights's influence on Jacobean drama criticism is so pervasive that he deserves at the least the honor of prior treatment. The common understanding of Middletonian comedy owes him much; sooner or later most studies mention the "economic revolution" or the "conflicting forces" that City Comedy portrays.

Knights's thesis is itself heavily influenced by the work of Weber and Tawney, who hold that cataclysmic religious disorders in the sixteenth century played a large part in changing social and economic conditions. In their view the paternalistic, relatively otherworldly outlook of Roman Catholicism was abandoned after the Reformation. Men began to value the fulfillment of worldly duties as the highest form of individual morality, an attitude that gave rise to the notion of a worldly vocation or calling.[23]

Calvin's teachings de-institutionalized Christianity. If no outward things helped man to salvation, the need for the Church, or for any other institution, was obviated. Left to himself, the individual was faced with an inexorable alternative: his predestined, inexplicable chosenness or eternal damnation. Confronted with the terrible tension this situation entailed, the Calvinist had to establish the conviction of his own salvation. Good works, though they availed nothing for salvation, could signify election. The Calvinist found himself driven into a life that would constantly assure him of his saintliness. He conducted himself carefully, striving to maintain the appearance of conviction of grace; he emphasized work and efficiency, abhorred laziness. Amassing of physical capital indicated entries on the credit side of the heavenly ledger, a belief remarkably congenial to commercial occupations. Calvinism developed into a middle-class movement accenting such middle-class virtues as dedication, industry, and sobriety. Individual initiative was a

---

23. Max Weber, *The Protestant Ethic and The Spirit of Capitalism*, trans. Talcott Parsons (London, 1930), p. 80.

virtue, and hard work a sign of the godly. So it was that land was commercialized and projects and monopolies multiplied.

These developments had their negative aspects. When man makes spiritual and physical needs congruent, the more carnal and rapacious side of his nature can easily come to dominate his outlook. By Middleton's day, says Tawney, "nature" referred to human appetites rather than divine ordinance; and the age's individualism gave natural rights as a reason for unleashing self-interest.[24]

Hence, Knights tells us, in late Elizabethan and early Jacobean England a new "acquisitive" middle class was elbowing aside its conservative, passive, rather flabby and old-fashioned betters. The Calvinist *bourgeoisie* was better equipped, in religious background and social position, to cope with a society rapidly becoming capitalistic. But economic methods changed before social thought. Older notions of class relationships, manners, and personal morality did not sit well with new theories of economic behavior. The more established classes, of course, adjusted their thinking to new conditions slowly. A major split between *bourgeoisie* and landed classes was represented on stage by the struggles of merchant villains against young gentry.

However, *Drama and Society* takes a rather simplistic view of the period, the forces shaping it, and the drama these forces affected. Throughout his book Knights is at pains to stress that the times were unique, that "the period was, peculiarly, a period of transition."[25] But all ages are times of transition, and it is not difficult to note a time's individuating characteristics, as Knights does, in order to demonstrate its uniqueness. Knights is perhaps too emphatic, as well, when he tells us what is distinctive about the years just before the "age of Jonson." He places the establish-

---

24. *Religion and the Rise of Capitalism* (New York, 1926), pp. 179–80.
25. Knights, p. 139.

ment of capitalistic processes then, as well as the emergence of money and competition, as primary factors in economic activity.[26]

Now, it can not be denied that conditions were changing in England under the last Tudor and first Stuarts, in ways that had not obtained previously. One prominent force for change was the dissolution of the monasteries in the second quarter of the sixteenth century, which transferred from ecclesiastical to lay hands a considerable portion of the country's land.[27] Others included the debasing of the coinage under Henry VIII and Edward VI, and a prolonged price rise, especially severe in the middle decades of the sixteenth century. Landlords, caught with an antiquated and unresponsive rent system, did what they could to modernize.[28] The more perceptive of them consolidated smaller plots, commercialized the home farm, enlarged the owner's demesne, and enclosed common ground. Some drained and cleared new land, others went into trade, exploiting timber and mineral resources. Foreign trade and domestic commerce had long been expanding.[29] The wool trade had called the guild system into being centuries before and had already outgrown it. As early as 1399, Henry IV had been expanding and confirming the "privileges" of the Company of Merchant Adventurers, as Edward III had done before him.[30] During the period of our concern the practice of

---

26. *Ibid.*, pp. 33 and 122.
27. William Ashley, *Economic Organisation of England*, 3rd ed. (London, 1949), p. 66. See also W. Cunningham, *The Growth of English Industry and Commerce*, Part 1, Vol. 2 (Cambridge, 1910) ; E. Lipson, *The Economic History of England*, 3rd ed. (London, 1943). The dissolution may not have been so radical a change as it is some times represented to be. See Geoffrey Baskerville, *English Monks and the Dissolution of the Monasteries* (New Haven, 1937), chaps. 2 and 4, esp. pp. 96–103.
28. This material is drawn from R. H. Tawney, "The Rise of the Gentry, 1558–1640," *EHR* 11 (1941) : 1–38.
29. Ashley, p. 95.
30. John Wheeler, *A Treatise of Commerce*, ed. George Burton Hotchkiss (New York, 1931), p. 321.

monopoly grew, as did its abuses. Small masters were gradually forced out of trades and the general public found itself buying high-priced, protected goods.

Almost everyone concedes that it was not the best of times for the established classes. Lawrence Stone recently detailed the maladies the aristocracy suffered.[31] Their most pressing problem was a decline in the regard once the aristocracy's due. Soon after his accession, James had initiated a needed reform by enlarging the peerage, which Elizabeth had neglected to maintain. But reform soon degenerated into abuse as James began to market titles.[32] Inflation of the aristocracy's numbers, crude methods of sale, and carelessness in examining the standing of purchasers all helped to undermine respect for the Crown and nobility.

The aristocracy also suffered from a number of debilitating vices. The nobleman led a life of extraordinary comfort and leisure. He spent lavishly on hunting, racing, travel, dowries, education, hospitality, housing, and service.

Life was prodigal in the country, even more carefree in the city. When Middleton started to write, London was the first and only city in England. Influenced by the lavishness of James's court, the City became a center of fashion. A season of sorts began to emerge, and litigation became a favorite sport. Throne, drawing room, and bench all had their part in attracting an ever-increasing flood of nobility to London.

Some feel, and Knights would probably be among them, that the nobility added an internal defect to hazards of station. As a class they were old and tired. The somnolence

---

31. *The Crisis of the Aristocracy 1558–1641* (London, 1965). The material for the following paragraphs is largely drawn from this source. See also Tawney, "Rise"; Lawrence Stone, "The Anatomy of the Elizabethan Aristocracy," *EHR* 18 (1948):1–53; H. R. Trevor-Roper, "The Elizabethan Aristocracy: An Anatomy Anatomized," *EHR*, 2nd ser. 3 (1950):279–98; *The Gentry 1540–1640*, The Economic History Review Supplements, 1, n.d.

32. Chapman, Marston, and Jonson incurred the Crown's wrath for their remarks on the selling of knighthoods in *Eastward Ho!* There are occasional references to "Scottish Knights" in Middleton's plays, and in others'.

that accompanies wealth and power had caught up with them. They were fated to be shunted aside by younger, atraditional gentry—smaller landholders, rich merchants, government officials, and professional men—who understood capitalistic practices and would use them.

Assessments of the significance of these events differ. Many historians do not hold either that the "acquisitive middle classes," to use Knights's phrase, were the exclusive cause of turmoil and upset or that they were chiefly responsible for the evils of the time. They disagree with Knights's picture of a war to the death between two irreconcilable forces. For Tawney, the heavy-laden galleons of the aristocracy ran aground, and the middle class salvaged the wreckage.[33] His metaphor seems more picturesque than accurate. One need not adopt the dialectical orientation of Knights and his followers. At least one historian, G. M. Trevelyan, objects specifically to Tawney's view of the nature of the trends of the sixteenth century, from which Knights draws considerable comfort.[34] He particularly opposes Tawney's idea that the sixteenth century was a watershed from which everything slid more and more rapidly downhill toward the large estates and landed farms of this century and the last one. By Trevelyan's reckoning, the consummation of economic and social change might well be placed late in the eighteenth century, in George III's time. H. R. Trevor-Roper feels that the established classes may have been healthier than Professor Stone believes. He also calls into question Tawney's evidence on the precipitous rise of the middle class.[35]

---

33. Tawney, "Rise," p. 27.
34. *English Social History* (London, 1944), p. 96.
35. Trevor-Roper, "The Elizabethan Aristocracy," p. 284. He objects to many of Stone's representations. Feeling that Stone does not understand Elizabethan loan machinery, Trevor-Roper states that he has "greatly exaggerated the indebtedness of the Elizabethan aristocracy." See also *The Gentry*, p. 46, where Trevor-Roper accuses Tawney of skewing his samples and of failing to present sufficient hard evidence to prove his point.

Relatively little structural change took place in English society between the fourteenth and nineteenth centuries. The roles of the various classes fluctuated, and within a fairly static framework.[36] Meanwhile, as Knights admits, the typical theatergoer came from a remarkably homogeneous background.[37] Images of class warfare do not do justice to the social reality. Class divisions existed and were duly recognized, with little fuss from any quarter. Heredity was not a radically determinant factor in social status. Individuals and families moved from class to class through gain or loss of property or even by change of occupation.[38] There was little significance, except for the mover, in which direction he tended. No great gulf was fixed between merchant turned squire and squire turned merchant. Of course, to use the terms *rising middle class* or *rising gentry* is itself misleading. Only a small percentage of individuals moved out of any particular class. The great majority were happy to remain where they were, as their fathers had done before and their sons would do after them.[39]

Turn-of-the-century social mobility can be seen as merely part of a constant historical process. For hundreds of years the higher classes had been receiving transfusions of money and blood from the ranks of the wealthier merchants. The movement of affluent merchants and industrialists on to the land, the downfall of decayed aristocrats, and the linking of nobility with money through marriage were hardly new.[40]

The business outlook was largely the same for all.[41] Landed men and moneyed men might talk as if they were rivals, but blood and interest made them allies. On the whole, older houses were no less progressive commercially

---

36. Stone, *Crisis,* pp. 5 and 671.
37. Knights, pp. 140–41.
38. Trevelyan, p. 162.
39. Trevor-Roper, *The Gentry,* p. 9.
40. J. H. Hexter, *Reappraisals in History* (Evanston, 1961), p. 80. See also Trevelyan, p. 126; Trevor-Roper, *The Gentry,* p. 24.
41. S. T. Bindoff, *Tudor England* (London, 1950), p. 36; Wheeler, p. 317.

than those more recently established.[42] Aristocrats and merchants were engaged in the same businesses and had the same problems. Economic shipwreck was no respecter of classes.

Even in such matters as speculation, the middle class knew its place. Though a good deal of investment capital came from the City, the upper classes stood security for risky new business ventures. After this first step, mercantile capital could be drawn into projects. The preponderance of those interested in projects were courtiers and their dependents or agents.[43] The landed classes also set the style for the volume and nature of consumer demand.

On the whole the middle class was docile. Some of its members were anxious, however, to leave the middle class. Ambitious merchants did not feel an urgent need to stay merchants; a family need not be perpetually "in trade." Class struggle demands some feeling of identity among class members, conditions that create solidarity. There must be irreconcilable differences in manner and viewpoint, coupled with little chance for social mobility. But in Stuart England, at least through Middleton's time, few new men except yeomen made their fortunes from land, although many hastened to turn their cash into landed estates as soon as they could. Such transactions were not astute business ventures. Land is a solid investment but normally a conservative one. The merchant land-buyer could have profited much more from speculation or trade than from the purchase of prestigious real estate. Merchants were not locked in a death grip with the aristocracy. They were standing in the outer chamber, cash in hand, diffident but not obsequious, trying to buy their way in, and were willing to pay a premium to do it.[44]

42. Hexter, pp. 78–85.
43. George Unwin, "Commerce and Coinage," *Shakespeare's England*, ed. C. T. Onions (Oxford, 1916), 1:335.
44. Hexter, p. 97.

In 1603 England was still predominantly medieval in economic and social organization. The country was agricultural; eighty percent of the people lived on the land. Even the enclosure phenomenon may not have been the complex reorganization of the countryside some consider it.[45] Change was on the way, but approaching gradually, as it usually does outside times of cataclysm.[46] Capitalistic processes had been in formation as early as Chaucer's day;[47] the social revolution had been a long time coming, indeed.

It seems difficult to consider Jacobean England the scene of a simple struggle between money and land, new men and patricians, City and country; and more difficult to say that Middleton was attempting to portray such a world. It would be simplistic to call the middle class acquisitive and rapacious. If time were changing (and they were), they were changing for all. The upper classes engaged in the same commercial innovations as their social inferiors, reaped the same advantages, suffered the same setbacks. Moreover, the aristocracy were addicted to a number of conspicuous vices, which had much to do with their decline. They stumbled more than they were pushed.

We will see that life is much of a piece up and down the range of the social ladder Middleton presents. Morality is easy in the plays and social relations complex and shifting because the times themselves were uncertain—for everyone —and social realities were less simple than they are sometimes represented to be. New standards of conduct and ways of doing things were affecting all classes of society, creating uncertainty and confusion, giving men new reasons for that perpetual wish for the return of a simpler past. In the first years under James, conditions were not yet chaotic, but could be disconcerting—on all levels of society.

---

45. Compare Knights, p. 98, with Trevelyan, pp. 116–17.

46. Only gradually, for instance, did James's administration lose its grip. There was a good deal of continuity from Elizabeth's reign. See David Harris Willson, *King James VI and I* (New York, 1956), p. 333.

47. Louis B. Wright, *Middle Class Culture in Elizabethan England* (Ithaca, N. Y., 1958), p. 5.

III

How did Middleton choose to portray this world in which he lived? Many feel that he did it "realistically." He has been called "the man who, more than any of his fellow dramatists, can claim to be called a realist."[48] According to this theory, Middleton gathered his materials from the streets, walks, and taverns through which he passed and rendered them into drama as faithfully as possible. Now, Middleton does seem to have written more important comedies centered on life in London streets and taverns than his fellows. His plays have a feel for locale, a flavor of contemporaneity that *The Alchemist* and *The Dutch Courtesan* do not even try to achieve. Among Jacobean comedies only *Bartholomew Fair* rivals Middleton's major works in their emphasis on local color.

It seems obvious, then, that Middleton paid attention to "real life." But was he "realistic?" Knights, surprisingly, perhaps, takes exception to the notion that he was. He observes, quite tellingly, that Middleton shows us only commonplaces: gallants make love to citizens' wives and are likely to be in debt, lawyers are more avid for fees than for justice, cutpurses are thieves. But Middleton does not give us individuals set in a particular time or place.[49] Few, however, have paid much attention to Knights's "discovery"; only lately have some begun to question the doctrine of Middletonian realism. Generally even the latest editors and critics tend to stand with critical tradition, though some attempt to modify the term *realistic* from time to time, giving it one meaning here, another there.[50]

This response is eminently understandable, even if it gives us a less than precise idea of what Middleton was about. All literature confronts reality in some way, if only

48. R. C. Bald, "The Sources of Middleton's City Comedies," *JEGP* 33 (1934) : 373.
49. Knights, p. 258.
50. For example, see *Michaelmas Term,* ed. Levin, p. xiv; Gibbons, p. 17; Holmes, pp. 39–40.

to propose its absurdity or nonexistence. The comic mode is said to be more realistic than the tragic, since it traditionally deals with "real life" or everyday events and characters. Comic characters do not use the exalted language suited to the lofty sentiments that once were the coin of tragedy. Their earthier language applies to quotidian concerns: money, food, sex, shelter, friendship. In this sense, comedy, including Middletonian comedy, is "realistic."

But the term actually has no business being applied to Middleton, has, in fact, distorted our perceptions of the artist. To call Middleton a "realist" we must overlook some basic facts. The doctrine of literary realism evolved long after Middleton wrote; and Jacobean writers, notorious borrowers that they were, lived and worked in a literary rather than a scientific age. Middleton was 300 years dead before realism emerged as a literary movement. Nineteenth-century Europe saw the rise of realism and then naturalism in the novel, and of the *bourgeois* stage conventions that so influenced Ibsen and the earlier Strindberg. Significantly, the notion of a "realistic" Middleton received its greatest currency during the twenties and thirties of this century, when the movement flourished.

Now realism evokes images of Zola with his tape measure and notebooks; the solid, accurately furnished stage set; playwrights detailing life in all the gritty detail the audience might notice on its way to the theater. The last image is the only one that half fits Middleton. It is beyond doubt that his characters are usually "low," both morally and socially. They are neither refined nor scrupulous. The plays abound with schemes, crimes, and concern over the most elemental needs of human life. These actions take place before a backdrop of references to places, times, and things familiar to Londoners of Middleton's day. There are allusions to events such as new coinages, occasional swipes at Scotland and at James's peddling of knighthoods, and mention here and there of unsavory suburbs like Brentford, Barn Elms, and Ware.

But these references do not amount to an attempt to give us a photographic reproduction of Jacobean City street life. In fact, relatively few references to the actualities of daily life (as opposed to purely literary allusions) have been positively identified. This is partially due to the passage of time, of course, but one wonders if Middleton was only trying to gain the same type of peripheral relevance that modern Shakespearean producers achieve when they put Henry V in hockey pads and give Hamlet a Hispanic accent. Jacobean audiences must have enjoyed these local references as much as we seem to enjoy seeing the familiar in our art forms. Fascination with the illusion of the present, with setting a story in familiar surroundings, seems constant in literature. Chaucer's pilgrims traveled a well-known road. Dante's Hell is populated with his acquaintances. Rabelais stages one of the Pantagrueline wars on his family's farm. The urge to localize literary themes, to clothe universal action in recognizable and congenial form, is natural, almost irresistible.

But the topical and the contemporary are not essential to humor. It is not central to our concern to discover who Ephestian Quomodo of *Michaelmas Term* is modeled on (if indeed he has a real-life model), because Quomodo is important primarily as a figure in a created comic context. Actualities incorporated into a play amuse us because they are used in a comic form, not because they are intrinsically humorous.[51] What E. H. Gombrich posits for the painter is equally true for the playwright. Jacobean writers, like all artists, were much more likely to draw on their stock of received schemata and types than they were to draw from the life.[52]

Middleton was answering demands with his plays, demands more basic than the aesthetic urge to get it down

51. Susanne K. Langer, *Feeling and Form* (New York, 1953), p. 347.
52. See Gombrich's interesting discussion in *Art and Illusion,* 2nd ed. (Princeton, 1961). Chaps. 2 and 7 are especially applicable to this problem. Gibbons refers to the study but in my opinion, does not make adequate use of it.

cold and hard and true. Like Shakespeare and others, Middleton was a commercial artist. Cash receipts were more important to him than the development of the capitalist system. He and his colleagues were entertainers; they devised works that they hoped would be successful enough to induce producers to continue to solicit their services. Over the years, certain figures, situations, and actions—comic conventions—had elicited laughter regularly because they enunciated something fundamentally human in experience, a congenial *irrationale* that leavened the drudgery and absurdity of human existence.[53] From these configurations of language and gesture Middleton borrowed, just as Shakespeare and Jonson did, and from them made something uniquely his own. A look at the possible sources of almost any of his plays, *Chaste Maid*, for instance, shows the considerable range of material Middleton ransacked. He filched from respectable forms as well as from such popular literature as rogue pamphlets, jest books, and other plays.[54] The Jacobeans were much more willing to accept the authority of the printed page than to do anything even faintly resembling the leg work of a Zola. Middleton was as great a borrower as any.[55]

Familiar elements served to make the audience fully at home with patterns of action thousands of years old. Middleton could play upon and manipulate attitudes toward current issues by applying surface characteristics—names, occupations, settings—to the constant patterns of comic human conduct. He worked in universals, giving his audience enough particulars to familiarize it with and interest it in his themes. Thus Middleton does imitate a reality in the

---

53. For an illuminating discussion of the function of convention in comic drama, and especially in Shakespeare's late romances, see Northrop Frye, *A Natural Perspective* (New York, 1965).

54. See *Chaste Maid,* ed. R. B. Parker (London, 1969), pp. xxxv–xxxix.

55. By now, Middleton's borrowings are well documented. See David George, "Thomas Middleton's Sources: A Survey," *N. & Q.,* n.s. 18 (1971): 17–24, which serves as reference to nearly all the previous work on the subject.

plays, the constant reality of traditional comic patterns. Only the most boring literature remotely approaches real life in its lack of action, gaps, silences, tentativeness, and essential blandness. Conversely, Middleton's plays bustle with life, brimful of characters—generally the same character types, doing the same things—who are always in action, always moving at high speed.

Middleton, then, was a sociologist only as much as is any artist possessed of creative insight. Like other writers of his time, he took his dramatic materials from the sources available to him, ransacking others' plays and his own earlier works, verse satire, rogue pamphlets, and jest books. Like Marston and Dekker, Middleton had worked in these forms before he came to drama, and he used these materials when he began to write plays.

Verse satire furnished a model chiefly for Middleton's less mature works. Since other considerations are involved in its study, it will be dealt with in the next section of this chapter. More immediately, the influence of the rogue pamphlet and jest book is apparent in all Middleton's comedies. The satiric plays, *The Family of Love, The Phoenix,* and *Your Five Gallants* are grab bags of incidents lifted almost bodily from pamphlet or joke collection; individual scrapes and jests are loosely contained within a satiric structure. Plays like *Michaelmas Term, A Trick,* and *Mad World* are much more unified. They show Middleton capable of working one or, at the most, two major incidents of the pamphlet type out to play length. In *Chaste Maid,* Middleton intertwines a number of stories and jests successfully, creating a whole vision of his comic society.[56] From first to last Middleton exhibits, as the rogue pamplets and jest books do, a sense of speed, a feel for colorful diction, a need to overstuff scene with character and incident. Middleton's young men, the rogues of the pamphlets, and the jokesters of the jest books generally act with the same

<hr>

56. Levin has noticed this. See *The Multiple Plot,* p. 218.

energy, wit, and insouciance. Each form has a thick, rich, heterogeneous texture characteristic not of life but of life raised to an abnormal pitch.

I could cite examples as sources or analogues of the plays; but it seems better to examine quality of influence rather than quantity. The pamphlets are responsible for something negative, the ersatz moral tone that permeates the satirical plays as well as pamphlets like Greene's *A Notable Discovery of Cozenage.* That work's patches of moral commentary remind one of the "redeeming social value" sections of our seamier contemporary films. Like the plays, the pamphlets were entertainments, and Greene was more interested in producing something salable than he was in excoriating vice. But Renaissance critical theory held that literature should instruct as well as delight, and the pamphlet was not too humble to feel it might justify itself. "Read and be warnd, Laugh as you like, Judge as you find," Greene admonishes on the title page of *The Black Book's Messenger.* But it takes us only a few pages to judge which clause is operative. Greene, who could not forget that he was a University man, may have wanted to justify this kind of writing to himself as well as to his audience. Middleton's plays also suffer from patches of didacticism thrown into the narrative, and his moralizing has the same spurious tone.

The moral lessons give the plays a disjointed air and bring the action to a standstill. For this and other reasons the comedies—the early satires much more than the ironic plays—suffer from loose structure. Play and pamphlet both have a tendency to include as many elements as possible, and not always in discernible order. The pamphlets intentionally, the early plays probably by accident, tend to be *mélanges* of incidents rather than patterned wholes.

But not all the correspondences are negative ones. The prose pamphlets are written in virile, racy prose, studded with Anglo-Saxon vocabulary. The language is vigorous, flexible, sometimes slangy and always figurative, above all earthy and elemental. We will see how vigorous and colloquial Middleton's language can be in the discussion of the plays.

Middleton's use of locale has already been discussed. The pamphlets also mass details for verisimilitude, but their illusion of reality is as superficial as the plays'. And the attempt at verity does not extend to characterization. The rogues and dupes of the pamphlets are types even more than are the characters of the drama. There is little attempt to give them individual personality or identity.

One character, akin to the Juvenalian satirist *persona,* seems almost a direct link with the drama, especially with the satiric plays—the narrator who operates within the story. He can be a criminal who recounts the villainies he watched and practiced (as in *The Black Book's Messenger*) or a citizen who saw crimes committed as he traveled around the city (as in Dekker's *The Bellman of London* and *Lantern and Candlelight*). We will see that Middleton at first used a similar character as the presenter of his satiric plays. The role disappeared in the more mature plays, since it tended to impede dramatic movement. But during his short career, the dramatic presenter acted as the narrator of the pamphlets did, observing individual scenes and jests, and stopping the action occasionally to lament the world's evils and the collapse of morality in a singularly wicked age. Although the movement is halting, individual pamphlet incidents are well conceived. Rogue pamphlet material could be staged easily, because the vignettes are often shaped dramatically or melodramatically; some are even written in dialogue form.

The characters who act within this semi-dramatic scheme could be transferred bodily to the stage play. In pamphlet and play, the characters not only want the same things but are the same types of people. Middleton's witless heirs, lecherous wives, crooks, and shrewd merchants could trade places with Greene's unsuspecting yokels, lecherous wives and whores, thieves and shrewd moneylenders.

The pamphlet form is essentially *bourgeois*. The qualities the writers praise and the rogues threaten, are peace, tranquility, honesty, and industry, prerequisites for a healthy business climate. Villains in pamphlets threaten goods, not lives; thievery and fraud, bane of merchant and prosperous burgher, are the only crimes committed. Prostitution, the commercialization of the flesh, is also a factor, usually in connection with fraud. Dupes become dupes because they are idle or because they try to cheat others themselves. At times the heavens visit the most incomprehensible of fates on the industrious merchants and citizens of the pamphlets: they are robbed or cozened of their hard-won goods for no reason, almost because they are without fault. The sites of the crimes—the walks of the city, ordinaries, bowling greens, even the playhouses—are exactly the types of places the citizen would frequent.

These are the places, too, where the characters of Middleton's plays gather, characters interested in the same kinds of pursuits and also fearful of losing goods and property. For Middleton's plays are fundamentally just as *bourgeois* in form as the pamphlets, and over the whole range of character. Merchant or gentry, Middleton's creatures have the same middle-class outlook, possibly because the playwright himself was allied by birth, occupation, and propensity to middle class *mores*. Consider any group of his comic characters: Yellowhammer, Allwit, Easy, Quomodo, Whorehound. In many ways they are hard to tell apart, guller or gulled, cutpurse or coney. With their common aspirations, manners of speech, and cheerful lack of scrupulosity, all are interested in amassing enough goods, money, or lands to lead a serene, comfortably materialistic life.

But the most important point of contact between the two forms is a matter of spirit. Both delight in what they purport to expose and condemn. The readers of the pamphlets were interested, in the main, precisely in the immoral adventures of the rogues, incredibly able, lucky, and villainous as they were. The pamphlets were read for entertainment, and it is not surprising that the same things still entertain today. Though the form is much more sophisticated, detective stories and crime *exposés* are not unrelated to Elizabethan popular literature. The plays employed the same materials and evoked the same fascinations. Middleton found he had to eliminate the moralizing almost entirely, because it stood in the way of the action that gives body to his comedy. In the more successful plays, as in the pamphlets, we admire the skill and exuberance of the tricksters and the *ingenium* of an artist who could shape such complicated schemes. One of the major attractions of Middletonian comedy is the sheer ability of the rogues to carry out their clever maneuvers.

The rogue pamphlets are also linked to the Elizabethan jest books in several ways.[57] There are similarities in plotting, character, purpose, and at times, in structure. The jest books influenced the drama directly as well as through the pamphlets. Middleton borrowed a good deal of material from the jest books; but, again, specific examples are not so important as more general questions of patterns and tone. What has been said about the pamphlets' flavor and texture applies equally well here. A number of specific traits correspond specifically with characteristics of Middleton's plays.[58] Characters in the jest books are rarely conscious or experienced sinners. They do little deliberate mischief; their insubordination can be construed as foolishness rather than cynicism or defiance. Actions are more playful than serious. They often fall into tightly structured patterns, often balanced, sometimes tripartite. The jokes often come

---

57. Joanna Brizdle Lipking, *Traditions of the* Facetiae *and Their Influence in Tudor England* (Columbia Ph.D. diss., 1970), p. 20.
58. *Ibid.*, pp. 193–240.

to an abrupt end, a *dénouement* that reveals the jest's two basic concerns: a sense that there must be a *quid pro quo* and a desire not only to answer but to punish. Like the pamphlets, the jests frequently offer morals, but their didacticism tends to be more sincere than either pamphlet's or play's.

Of course, it is possible that the jokesters, the pamphleteers, and Middleton all went directly to real life and shaped it into literature from the same educational and social stance. It has been suggested that jest books were a much more respectable form than is often thought. They emerged from the humanist tradition; jest material was not deemed unworthy by such serious writers as More, Latimer, and Harington. Middleton, a University man, may have structured experience as the pamphleteers did because of similar training. But it seems better to say that dramatist, pamphleteer, and joke collector were writing in the same conventional mode, using the same literary sources, giving their works the same patina of realism. For the most part, these writers were trained in a tradition that put a premium on imitation, the attempt not to ape but to overgo literary models. It seems doubtful that they would bother to forge their own plots from the mess of daily life when congenial sources like pamphlets and jest books, skillfully shaped accounts of dramatic interplay, sometimes even in dramatic form, were at hand, ready for pillaging.

An examination of *A Game at Chess* produces some evidence for this contention. This work, the only one of Middleton's that we know deals in large part with contemporary characters and events, was the most successful draw in English Renaissance drama. It ran for nine consecutive performances before being closed by government order and owed both its success and its demise to its "realism." Under the allegory of a game the play dealt with the proposed alliance of Prince Charles with a Spanish princess. Among its characters were figures resembling Charles, Buckingham,

James, the King of Spain, and Count Gondomar, the highly unpopular Spanish ambassador.

Middleton's known sources for the play, aside from real life, are a series of polemical religious pamphlets.[59] Literary sources, then, for a very "realistic" subject. And real life, we discover, makes a very poor play. *A Game at Chess* has little dramatic unity. Merely an assortment of rhetorical thrusts at the arch-villain Gondomar and the Spanish in general, the play is completely static. It has none of the continuous rush of the comedies. For this the source material, more rhetorical than dramatic in shape, is only partially responsible. Middleton, answering needs other than to amuse and entertain, was satirizing actual people involved in known actions. Real life pulled him out of his customary dramatic patterns. A feeling of aimlessness results, a sense that the characters are standing about, waiting to keep an appointment with a specific historical event.

More conventional comedies do not suffer such inhibitions. Their characters are driven about the stage. Familiar comic forces surge through the channels formed by centuries of comic writing and acting. In them, Middleton's traditional, stock material is fitted into stock, traditional patterns, the same basic configurations that served Aristophanes, Plautus, and Terence almost 2,000 years before. In *The Clouds, The Wasps,* and *A Trick to Catch the Old One,* the plot turns on the conflict between generations. In *Mad World,* Follywit jousts with a type of his father rather than with a rapacious merchant. The title story of *Chaste Maid* deals with the attempts of two young people to fool the girl's parents. Conflict in Middleton generally occurs between an older and a younger person. Witgood, Follywit, and the Touchwoods all find their ambitions impeded by older, unregenerate antagonists.

These characters and the actions in which they engage are literary, traditional, highly conventional. They fulfill

59. George, p. 22.

Cornford's prediction that the Young Man, a secondary character in Aristophanes, would have a brilliant career, overshadowing that of his morose, stingy parent.[60]

IV

If one challenges the conventional wisdom about Middleton's realism and the socioeconomic background of his plays, other facets of the criticism become suspect, notably the notion that his plays are satiric.

Satire, probably the most topical, realistic comic genre, was quite the vogue in England during the 1590s. Middleton participated in the movement, although he was too young to play a sizable role.[61] Thomas Nashe, John Donne, Joseph Hall, and John Marston were some of the major writers who responded to an increasing fascination with classical satire by trying their hand at writing imitations, usually in verse. Over the years the satirist had come to be pictured as a shaggy, uncouth, misanthropic figure (a satyr), who raged and snarled at the world. Writers aped the *saeva indignatio* of Juvenal, the epitome of the perfect satirist. As the decade came to a close, satiric activity became especially scurrilous and biting. The growing indecency and harshness ended abruptly June 1, 1599, when the Bishop of London ordered several satirical works burned, including one of Middleton's, and banned the printing of satires and epigrams.

The evils of censorship aside, it was probably fortunate that the authorities found satire intolerable; it did not seem to thrive in "the fresh air of an essentially rural economy"

---

60. Francis Cornford, *The Origins of Attic Comedy,* ed. Theodore H. Gaster (Garden City, 1961), p. 149.

61. See Alvin Kernan, *The Cankered Muse* (New Haven, 1959); also O. J. Campbell, *Comicall Satyre* (San Marino, Cal., 1938); John Peter, *Complaint and Satire in Early English Literature* (Oxford, 1956); Robert C. Elliott, *The Power of Satire* (Princeton, N. J., 1960); Anthony Caputi, *John Marston, Satirist* (Ithaca, N. Y., 1961).

where "the moral atmosphere was still clean."[62] Elizabethan verse satire, essentially a a hothouse plant, has been viewed as an attempt, often made by precocious youth, to write poems as much like newly discovered classical epigrams and satires as possible.[63] Elizabethan satirists did not write out of deeply offended sensibility; they were fully, quietly aware of their actions and aims. Marston's efforts, to give only one example, have been called an almost "pretentious" attempt to elevate the genre.[64]

Though John Peter indicates that satire continued as a distinctive form after the edict,[65] it is beyond debate that Marston and Middleton devoted their main energies to the drama. There they, along with Jonson, wrote plays marked by the verse satire experience. Jonson's *Poetaster* is a good example of the self-consciousness that marked the drama of the day in and out of the *poetomachia*. Though not so bitter as the poetry, the early plays were just as carefully didactic. Middleton's first dramatic steps matched Marston's and Jonson's. All employ a character who oversees and sometimes guides the action, in hiding or disguise; loose structure; didactic tone; and condemnation and harsh punishment of the misdeeds on display. At this point in its development, Jacobean comedy was far too static, though the means for putting it in motion were not lacking. It debated issues or attacked people and points of view much as Aristophanes attacked Socrates and Euripides, though with less grace and without real verve.

Satire did not take to the stage easily; it seldom does. Drama is a communal activity. A member of a theater audience must discard his individuality to a degree, share in the common awareness of his fellow spectators. The play imposes similar restrictions on the dramatist, who must

---

62. James R. Sutherland, *English Satire* (Cambridge, 1958), p. 30.
63. Peter, p. 112.
64. Caputi, p. 50.
65. Peter, pp. 152ff.

address a commonality rather than a group of disparate individuals and so tends to employ the most catholic standards possible. The complications of this for satire are telling; objects of attack become general, and the immediacy of criticism slips away entirely.[66] As the new playwrights acquired a sense of what would go on stage, faults and situations became less serious, patches of didacticism shrank, and the hidden or disguised presenter, at least in Middleton, merged into the action and eventually disappeared as a dramatic device.

It is inaccurate simply to call Middleton's plays "satires." His early works do show satirical tendencies. But satire is militant irony. It employs relatively clear moral norms and assumes definite standards for measuring the grotesque and absurd.[67] As stage comedy's norms became more general and consequently more fuzzy, Middleton's plays—never purely satiric, having no clear or well-defined standards of judgment—became more and more purely ironic. And his ironic comedy is far from being amoral or didactic. Middleton employs irony without abandoning the attempt to create a moral vision of man and society, an artistic moral vision that even his satires reflect, however confusedly. The impression of Middleton's lack of artistic balance, the notion of even his "misanthropy" exists only because City Comedy has not been adequately examined as part of the main stream of English comedy.

We should have some notions about the nature of comedy clearly in mind when we discuss a particular comedian's work; this chapter has been necessary because too many commentators have failed to do just that in Middleton's case. Comedy is a form of play, an activity out of the ordinary, absented from what we call real life. The comic realm has a disposition all its own; it generates a special logic, a

---

66. *Ibid.*, pp. 196–97.
67. Northrop Frye, *The Anatomy of Criticism* (Princeton, N. J., 1957), p. 223.

distinctive set of values. Suffused as its actions are with
release from the strictures of ordinary normative behavior,
comedy possesses an essential joyousness and gusto, however biting it may be on the surface. Pleasure springs even
from the ability to say the hurtful thing, since it is enunciated in a world where it will not and cannot wound as it
otherwise might.[68]

Comedy's abandoning of the real world is tied to an
awareness of its own artificiality. It possesses a limited but
twofold knowing, for it is aware at once of its freedoms
and the limitations that circumscribe them. It knows how
much is permitted its stock characters within the well-defined
rules and boundaries of comic situation, but knows as well
that these boundaries, in the context of life itself, are only
secondarily real and frequently are absurd. As Freud points
out, the question of prolonging play's pleasure is at the heart
of the comic jest. The joke must not only amuse but also
silence critical objections that would not allow pleasureable
feelings to emerge. To do this, the joke plays the game of
the serious: it constructs absurd words and thoughts so that
they have a meaning, even if a nonserious one. The jocose
statement has the value a serious comment must have if it
is to be accepted, although the value is one stood on its
head.[69]

But at last the joke ends. The joker and his listener return
to a more serious, essentially tragic order of being. This
unavoidable return is partially responsible for the bad press
comedy is prone to receive. As a construct that deals with
life at arm's length, comedy can easily be considered less
serious and less "valuable" than tragedy, which seems to
meet life head on. But comedy is a worthwhile mode of perception. On its own terms and in its own way, it deals with

68. This and the following paragraphs owe much to Johan Huizinga,
Homo Ludens (Boston, 1955), chap. 1.
69. Sigmund Freud, *Jokes and Their Relation to the Unconscious,* ed. and
trans. James Strachey (New York, 1963), pp. 129-31.

life and the desire for it, with the freedom and mobility that unencumbered life entails.

Real comedy produces in its audience a sense of general exhilaration. It presents something inevitably exciting, the very image of livingness. The story inevitably deals with a temporary triumph over the real world, complicated and stretched out by a series of coincidences. The stage-life of comedy has a rhythm of feeling transmitted to us by our perception of a whole familiar world moving into its future. We laugh at the high points of a life abstracted and composed but still recognizable as our own, a life universally human and impersonal.[70]

An element of comedy's universal humanity is its preoccupation with a constant object of human experience: the material. Comedy starts at the beginning, quite literally and concretely, with phallus and female earth. It is unafraid of the instruments and symbols of its begetting. Like other comedians, Middleton has often been castigated because his works do not hesitate to mention their origins. But comedy got its start around the Maypole,[71] and Middleton could hardly escape it and remain a comedian.

Comedy emerges from the material, but does not deal with it simplistically. It does not pay heed only to the body's members or functions, just as life is not known only in the body. Comedy is acquisitive. It desires to amass things, just as we come to know we are alive only when and as we confront the other. Hence comedy's overwhelming interest in objects, in greed and the desire to cram the world down gullets and hoard it in rooms.[72]

Amassing of objects is a repetitive activity, and laughter fights the repetitive, the intrusion of the mechanical into human life. Henri Bergson speaks of the comic as that

70. Langer, p. 348.
71. Gilbert Murray, *The Classical Tradition in Poetry* (Cambridge, Mass., 1927), p. 50.
72. Eric Bentley, *The Life of the Drama* (New York, 1964), p. 304.

which shows a person's likeness to a thing, that element of sameness in human events that betrays a certain inelasticity or automatism, movement without life. Laughter both defends against this and serves as a corrective for it. This distinctly human physiological activity seeks to chastise those who treat social relations as things. It punishes those who no longer concern themselves with the vital reciprocal system that is society.[73]

The young scamp triumphs, obtains girl or gold, or both, because he more than any other character sees what courses are viable amid the materialistic chaos of the play world. In the end he breaks out of the cycle of the acquisitive impulse by foreswearing further involvement in his customary pursuits. This triumph over the world of matter, signified by the acquisition of goods, would be impossible without the use of intellect. The comic hero uses his head to overcome the prevailing "rational" order of things. Comedy does not attack reason *per se,* but abuses of the rational faculty: regimentation, law's failure to be adequately particular or even just, custom's resistance to accommodation to change. It opposes the mechanization and dehumanization of the world through the continuous encroachments of what we call civilization. Comedy, then, affords us a needed balance for the oppressive products of over- or false intellection. It strives to protect the irreducible element of irrationality in the human make-up. When we observe comedy's stock characters or engage in its stock actions, we defeat the mechanical at its own game. In becoming a puppet or enjoying a puppet's motions, we indulge in the outrage of irrationality but are spared its consequences.[74]

Comedy's crowding, mechanization, speed, and use of types are calculated ways to return to childhood, to the indivisibility of experience. The spirit rebels against the

---

73. "Laughter," in *Comedy,* ed. Wylie Sypher (Garden City, 1956), p. 117.
74. Bentley, p. 222.

frequently arbitrary nature of distinctions between good and bad, permissible and forbidden. It resents the surrender of personal autonomy to social demands. As such, comedy can be both subversive and defensive. At times comedy fights a holding action, making things endurable. It can be the distancing agent that holds at arm's length not just rationality and civilization but more specific hurts as well. Comic themes are inherently painful or vexatious. They involve pain that distresses us moderately but chronically, discomfort that laughter lets us endure and, at moments, overcome.[75]

Comedy, then, can be at once concerned and unconcerned with society. It takes us out of the ambiguity of the real world into a realm of definite rules and pace. Participants in the comic world do what is impossible or unconscionable in social life. Comedy defends against that from which it takes its being, for it is life, but at a remove in pace, clarity, and complexity. It cannot escape completely from the actualities of existence, nor does it want to, because it is a commentary on them.

It is somewhat hasty to define a comic writer's moral vision before one has considered the special moral configuration his comedy generates. It is just as hasty to condemn a writer for dealing with the basics of human existence before observing the use to which he puts fundamental urges and desires. Middleton, I feel, employs them to create an ironic picture, highly stylized, highly complicated, of the Jacobean world. Irony expresses the basic duality of comedy, its desire both to engage an audience in laughter and to afford it a respite from the rigors of social life. Middleton employs it to express and resolve his own duality, the attraction and repulsion he apparently felt for the life his works depicted. He saw that his traditional, literary materials ran in patterns that corresponded to basic configura-

---

75. Ramon Fernandez, *Molière*, trans. Wilson Follett (New York, 1958), pp. 136–37.

tions of contemporary life, and used them to mirror both its positive and negative aspects.

It was perhaps inevitable that he would rely on irony as his basic tool, since it is so inevitably a dual mode of perception, having at its core the notion of saying one thing while meaning another. Fernandez calls it "a species of absence while present that sunders more hopelessly than actual isolation." To treat someone seriously is to be at one with him; to treat him comedically is to be at two with him.[76] At two with him, not against him. Irony does not isolate as satire does, with its definite moral norms and clear, aggressive sense of right and wrong. Satire approaches actuality in that it proposes, explicitly and implicitly, standards of conduct for real people in real situations. But irony does not confront reality; it flirts with it by indirection.

Drama is a mode of expression amenable to irony by its very nature. Stage irony entails the understanding of three distinct parties—speaker, person spoken to, and audience, which can understand more than either stage party and shares, to the extent it is permitted, in the Olympian overview of the author. If a situation is invariably comic when it belongs to two orders of events,[77] interjection of a third order increases the possibilities geometrically. One is not only at two with a person, but at two with him while being observed by another with his own point of view.

A playgoer is not a *tabula rasa*. He compares a comic piece, however implicitly and haphazardly, with some set of standards, an attitude toward experience that he employs in the real world. In determining the complexity of the comic response, one must take into account experience brought to the work as well as experience gained from it. The actual words reside in the play, and are spoken to characters who hear and misunderstand them. There misunderstanding is temporary, ending when the playwright

76. *Ibid.,* p. 117.
77. Bergson, p. 123.

wishes it. The effect on the audience is of a different order. The viewer understands both sides of an ambiguous statement. Inevitably, he will refer the implied and contradictory meanings of what he sees and hears to the standards that guide him in the real world. In turn, these standards and attitudes are referred back to the special rules and values comedy employs and compared with them.

Further complications ensue if the play's standards, while compromised by the existence of moral or idealistic norms outside the play, still seem viable. A double judgment follows: a readjustment of both standards toward a central norm somewhere between what occurs on stage and in the street. The theoretical purity of the standards of daily life becomes less significant when the viewer realizes that the tricky doings of comic characters, actions purged of dross by their very success, are in some ways valuable modes of action. What Huizinga postulates of the archaic mind is relevant to more sophisticated sensibilities. Winning is proof of truth and rightness.[78] If a rogue like Witgood outwits the old men in *A Trick,* he is "sanctified," to an extent, by his victory.

The standard of every day, unless totally compromised, will continue to be useful, and perhaps more useful, if we realize its flaws. For we cannot live by irony alone. We would not want to arrange our lives as Witgood, Follywit, and the Touchwoods do. The success of a strictly practical mode of behavior is something of a wish fulfillment, bodied forth in the figures of fantasy that populate the comic setting. They represent the release, the spirit of play that writer and audience would like to see in their everyday dealings. If only we could ignore the models on which we pattern our behavior—if we could cheat just a little, could outwit the pompous, dull characters who vex us, could do the outlandish things we long to do—how happy we feel we might be. But we know that such things are not reasonable or, ultimately, even desirable.

---

78. Huizinga, pp. 81–82.

V

So irony ends with a whimsical smile and sigh rather than the snarl of satire. It comes to terms with society instead of attacking it. It is not antisocial, but ultimately social. Instead of imputing malice it reminds us of our all-too-human imperfection. The butts of irony misunderstand not because of ill will or refusal to do the good, but because they are too wrapped up in themselves to function correctly. Even these egocentric characters are eventually drawn into comic society. Irony tells its victims it wishes they were intelligent enough to understand, to function in a world where ironic comment would be unnecessary.

We will see how Middleton moved from satiric frontal assault to indirect ironic commentary. In doing so he resolved difficulties in structure, tone, and meaning in his work, and came to accept the characters and situations he employed and the truths this material mirrored. As an artist, he was not interested in morality as a thing in itself, but rather in the whole range and structure of human activity. His ironic comedy deals not only with personal idiosyncrasies but with social, economic, and familial *mores*.

He used traditional materials to deal with universal problems. Character and incident were drawn in abundance from the preexistent materials of popular literature and dramatic tradition. Figures who were merely rogues in the pamphlets, ostensibly and ultimately springing from the Elizabethan underworld, eventually settled, on Middleton's stage, into older, more conventional patterns, the configurations of classical stage comedy. Rogues, sharpers, and con men assumed the features of irascible old men, types of the classical *senex*. The gull or coney became the *adulescens*, invariably put upon and held down by his parent. The resourceful and witty slave was reborn as well, sometimes as an unscrupulous servant, sometimes merged into the figure of the young man.

Middleton was concerned with the phenomena of chang-

ing times; he found, as others had before him, that irony
is especially suited to treat the problems caused by the co-
existence of two life styles, one waxing, one waning, each
an ironic commentary on the other.[79] He used irony to deal
with marriage, money and barter exchange, the law and
the courts, inheritance, and other political and customary
procedures that had or could become lifeless, abstract, inflexible, and mindlessly repetitious.

In treating them he did not simply dichotomize by placing
his characters in opposed camps. He used increasingly complex patterns of ironic action to deal with a complex social
situation. The irony works inside traditional character configurations as well as outside them. Within, "immoral"
characters, often young men, are able to break down barriers set up by their fathers and elders because they are able
to see the folly of law, pedantry, Puritan hyper-morality,
customs of inheritance, greed. They can do this because the
playwright has placed them in a world all their own, beyond
the pedestrian, quotidian world of relatives and creditors,
who pay lip service to convention and pervert it to justify
selfish and immoral schemes. The hypocrites consider the
young men fools and wastrels, which gives the "immoralists"
a chance to act unobserved and gain for themselves the
reasonable life they desire. Misguided conventional wisdom
rebounds back on itself at the end of the plays.

But often enough, the young are indicted as well as the
old. Countervailing patterns of action make their victories
less than complete. Youth finds it must engage in evil to
overcome evil, must use deceit to defeat aged hypocrisy.
Ultimately we are left with a portrait of a world full of
both good and evil, a place of complex and contradictory
motivation and sympathies, though Middleton assents to
his creation more than he rejects it.

---

79. Walter J. Kaiser, *Praisers of Folly* (Cambridge, Mass., 1963), p. 24.
This excellent study of Erasmus, Rabelais, and Shakespeare has much to
say about the nature of irony.

Of course, this is presented to best advantage in the mature, ironic comedies. Before we deal with them, however, we must examine the harsher, simpler picture of life presented in the satiric plays, which introduce many of the problems Middleton eventually solved.

2

The Satiric Plays

*T*HE *Family of Love* and *The Phoenix* are among Middleton's earliest works. *Your Five Gallants* may have appeared a few years later but is similar to them in satiric form, theme, and tone. Almost universally regarded as slight works—flat failures or only partial successes— they have provoked little critical comment. But a study of them will reveal how satire functions on stage, show what Middleton escaped in his better work, and shed light both on the origins of some virtues of his mature plays and on the disturbing moral duality that characterizes his comedy up to *Chaste Maid*.

Middleton's earliest, nondramatic works, especially *The Wisdom of Solomon Paraphrased* and *Micro-Cynicon,* are much concerned with the question of moral conduct, as are the satirical plays. *Micro-Cynicon* is a short—and curious— piece, but it does reveal something of the nature of satirical form. The work consists of a prologue introducing the satirist and six "snarling satires"; in each satire a figure illustrative of a particular vice is introduced and then excoriated by the harsh, unyielding satirist. Here, in embryo, we have the scheme of the early plays, where figures representing particular moral defects—crews as motley as *Micro-Cynicon*'s—are brought to bar by a figure who dominates the action when and as he wishes and mediates between action and audience, guiding the viewer's response.

The form is crude and simple, but held considerable fascination for a number of playwrights despite its resistance to being made stage worthy. Marston and Jonson also experimented with dramatizing this hero-observer, master of prosecution and revels. While Middleton was writing his early plays, Marston produced, among others, the Antonio plays, *The Fawn,* and *The Malcontent,* and Jonson *Every Man Out of His Humour, Cynthia's Revels,* and *The Poetaster.* Though they differ in other ways, these plays share as basic formal elements the dramatic satirist, or presenter, with his harsh impatience with evil. As time passed, the presenter declined in importance. He disappeared (as in *The Alchemist*) or was discredited (as in *Bartholomew Fair*) or survived in vestigial form, as in some of Middleton's brighter works. Middleton's efforts at involving the presenter in dramatic action will make clear the reason for the figure's demise. These plays suffer from a disparity between matter and form. Middleton finds it difficult here to forgive or understand evil; but the evil he finds most worthy of laughter is the stuff of more lighthearted comedy—the standard jests and tricks discussed earlier. We are torn between enjoying the humor—or seeing what we were meant to enjoy, when the jests are especially vapid—and being told we should condemn them.

Ultimately, the plays tell the story of a writer stymied by his material and his intent, unable, at moments, to reconcile his tendencies to accept human fallibility and condemn human wickedness.

The Family, probably Middleton's earliest extant comedy, was written soon after he left the university. A cursory glance reveals at work the hand of a young man intoxicated with his learning. The characters spout Latin, parse nouns, dwell on etymologies, and make copious allusions. The comedy's pedantic ingenuity is reminiscent of another early effort, *The Poetaster.*

The play's basic scheme, repeated in *The Phoenix* and *Your Five Gallants,* consists of placing a series of rather aimless jests and tricks within a frame-tale, which is held in suspension as the jokes are worked out in the body of the action. Middleton attempts to connect the two kinds of material by making the hero of the romantic plot the presenter of the follies of the jest characters, some of whom compete with him for the hand (and body) of his beloved.

Here Gerardine loves and wishes to marry Maria, but her guardian uncle, Dr. Glister, disapproves. He is disenchanted with Gerardine, whose fortunes are at low ebb, a malady common to Middleton's heroes. Glister also suspects him of inconstancy, although he does not support his accusation with evidence (I.i.3-5). The two lovers conspire to marry despite his opposition. Gerardine pretends to go on a trip, goes into hiding in Maria's room, and eventually tricks her guardian into allowing the match.

While Gerardine hides, the characters of the underplot play out their jokes and silly tricks, a few of which are aimed, rather haphazardly, at the religious sect of the title. Most consist of the mindless intrigues of fop gallants Lipsalve and Gudgeon and the amours of Mistress Purge, the only major figure who belongs to the Family of Love.[1] This lady is the key figure of the subplot, since she either dallies with or is attempted by every man in the play except Gerardine and her husband.

---

1. Bullen tells us the Family was an obscure sect founded by an Anabaptist in Holland before the midpoint of the sixteenth century. Middleton attacks none of the actual tenets of the faith that Bullen was able to discover. See *Works,* 3:4-5.

Other motifs, developed in later plays, are at least touched on here. Early in the play (II.i.1-23), Purge is the type of the wittol Allwit becomes in *Chaste Maid*. Lipsalve and Gudgeon forget each other as easily as Lethe does his companions in *Michaelmas Term*. Like the later plays this work involves more than a struggle over spouse and social position. It attempts satire, with the Puritan sects, their hypocrisy, and the manners of various social groups as targets. Merchants take their lumps as do fashionable gallants.

Gerardine is the observer-satirist, and he and Maria embody as well as register disapproval of the sins and crimes the other characters commit.[2] The world of Maria and Gerardine is distinguished by a moral tone completely different from that of the lecherous, deceitful groups around them. Middleton emphasizes this even stylistically. The lovers speak pious, frigid verse while the other characters use a bawdy but rather commonplace prose. Middleton is continuously at pains to stress the purity and nobility of his two lovers. Even in highly romantic love scenes, he forces on them the most precious of sentiments. Early, the lovers' purity is so emphasized that a character observing them must make the obligatory earthy comments that would sound incongruous coming from them:

> *Gerardine.* My dear Maria, be comforted in this:
> The frame of heaven shall sooner cease to move,
> Bright Phoebus' steeds leave their diurnal race,
> And all that is forsake their natural being,
> Ere I forget thy love.
> *Maria.* Who's that protests so fast?
> *Gerardine.* Thy ever-vowed servant, Gerardine.
> *Maria.* O, by your vows, it seems you'd fain get up.
> *Lipsalve.* Ay, and ride too.   (*Aside.*
> (I.ii.98–106)

---

2. But see Levin, *The Multiple Plot*, pp. 59–66. Levin is probably over-ingenious in seeing three levels of action. He thinks of the inconsequential pranks of Lipsalve and Gudgeon as a separate "plot" and overschematizes the moral hierarchy of the play.

The sterile verse halts the action whenever it crops up, as it often does. Even the characters' names emphasize the split in tone. The lovers have Christian appellations while all the others—Glister, Purge, Dryfat, Lipsalve, Shrimp, Periwinkle—have labels, usually derisive, that reveal an aspect of either their appearance or their occupation.

There are other significant differences between the two plots. Unlike the two faithful lovers, the other characters engage in a farrago of assignations, attempted seductions, and mindless lechery. The romantic story is static, the low plot full of chaotic action, a condition emphasized by the strategy Middleton uses to connect the stories. Gerardine employs the hoary coffin-trunk trick to gain access to Maria's room. Once there he does nothing for a good part of the play but watch unseen the indiscretions of the other characters. When he does go out among the low characters, he is disguised. Gerardine is always the observer, watching and commenting on the action. In his desire to force the viewer's attitude, Middleton places others in the role of hidden commentator also. Glister tricks Lipsalve and Gudgeon into whipping each other and furnishes moral commentary as they punish themselves for lechery. Disguised as a member of the Family, Purge sees his wife cuckold him with the merchant, Dryfat. The gallants' pages comment freely, in asides, on the stupidities of their masters. But none of these situations carry the moral weight of Gerardine's observation and control; he alone does not play a dual role by participating in the action as well as observing it.

Despite the play's satirical strategy and careful drawing of lines of behavior, its moral position is uncertain. Commentary is never localized. The low characters are obviously types, their foolish actions conventional. The vices themselves can be classified only under the most general categories. Far from holding a mirror up to nature, Middleton paints in the objects of derision with a few crude brush strokes.

The satire on the Family of Love is more than obvious. The sect is seldom at the center of the action; when it is, Middleton's unimaginative charge is that the members of this fanatically pure group indulge in free love in the sanctity of their meeting house. Mistress Purge insists on the utmost cleanliness at home but couples with anyone available after lights out at the Family's services.

Since Mistress Purge is the spouse of a merchant, some of the shafts are aimed at the proverbial promiscuity of the citizen's wife—more, of course, than a contemporary motif. Were she not a Puritan, Mistress Purge could change places with the miller's wife and daughter in Chaucer's "Reeve's Tale" or with similar figures in any number of traditional stories and jests. Though Middleton does poke fun at the merchant class, social boundaries mean little to his humor. Gallants take their falls also; Lipsalve and Gudgeon, types of the automatic courtier, epitomize lust and foolishness and seem almost born out of time. They would be perfectly at home in such an early, crude Restoration comedy as *Love in a Tub*.

Cupidity is not so major a target as lust, but it is also an object of attack. Glister is astonishingly greedy and Purge's "business sense" is remarkable, though by no means praiseworthy: he allows his wife to cuckold him at will so long as it benefits him financially.

After these ills have been exposed in an overlong, disjointed series of pranks, Gerardine, disguised as "Master Doctor Stickler," sets out to remedy them. In the judgment scene he purges the play world of evil, giving metaphorical value to the rather coarse image that dominates the play: physical purgation. The apothecary's name is Purge. Glister, whose name means clyster, a now-obsolete term for enema,[3] avenges the gallants' attempt to cuckold him by giving them an emetic. Mrs. Purge is constantly being "ministered to"

---

3. OED.

by Glister the master purger, and the gallants discover that
looseness of the flesh has multiple meanings:

> *Gudgeon.* She makes civil wars and insurrections
> in the state of my stomach: I had thought to have
> bound myself from love, but her purging comfits make
> me loose-bodied still.
> *Lipsalve.* What, has she ministered to thee then?
> *Gudgeon.* Faith, some lectuary or so.
>
> (II.iii.57–62)

The pervasive image of the comic underplot, then, is an
elemental one; and sexual urges, linked with other basic
needs of the body, have the same inevitability attributed to
them. Gerardine attempts to cleanse the low characters of
their base desires and succeeds to a degree with some. To
Lipsalve and Gudgeon he recommends the learning of the
"ABC of better manners." Mrs. Purge will find it more
difficult to deceive her husband, though there is a hint that
she will continue to do so. Even Glister's hidden vices are
brought to light, one by one.

The action of the play moves toward completion and
resolution. The strategy starts with a condition of original
evil, moves to a spying out of examples, and proceeds to a
final arraignment that entails confession, judgment, the
awarding of punishment, and a promise to reform, or at
least a look by the miscreant in that direction. By making
the wrongdoers aware of their faults, Gerardine attempts
to guide them to more healthy habits of personal and so-
cietal conduct. But the play is still very unsettling. Despite
his helping fulfill the formula, Gerardine, as observer-pre-
senter, does not form a satisfactory link between the two
plots. The play disintegrates because its two principal parts
are ill-suited to each other.

Middleton does attempt to equate the two actions, but
the effort seems singularly forlorn. Gerardine revenges him-

self on Glister by using a trick Glister himself might consider. Gerardine dallies with Maria during his stay in her
room—with results that become obvious during the play,
insinuates to Glister's wife that her husband is responsible,
and blackmails Glister into letting him marry Maria. Thus
the lovers achieve matrimony by using a trick that had not
even occurred to the low characters. Glister, Mistress Purge,
and the others are arraigned for their fleshliness; but Maria
and the prosecutor, Gerardine, practice carnality with a
vengeance—to the point of bringing new "flesh" into the
world.

At first glance this would seem to present an irony worthy
of Middleton's most mature comedies, where successful
characters constantly turn their opponents' weapons back
against them. But it does not work here. The efficacy of the
irony is lost because such a trick is simply inappropriate to
the personalities of the Gerardine and Maria we see. Middleton is at pains to show how different Maria and Gerardine
are from the other characters in the one activity in which
they could be most similar. The lovers merely go through
the motions; there is no joy for them in the trick, which is
carried out in the same cold, spiritless fashion as the rest
of their relationship.

Gerardine's approach to seduction is hopelessly bad:

> Hear me exemplify love's Latin word
> Together with thyself:
> As thus:—hearts joined, *Amore:* take *A* from thence,
> Then *more* is the perfect moral sense,
> Plural in manners, which in thee do shine
> Saint-like, immortal, spotless, and divine:
> Take *m* away, *ore* in beauty's name
> Craves an eternal trophy to thy fame:
> Lastly, take *O* in *re* stands all my rest,
> Which I, in Chaucer-style, do term a jest.
>
> (III.i.46–55)

This chilly, pedantic conceit sets the tone for the entire romance. But the fault lies more in Middleton's fundamental conception of the situation than in its tone. He does not want the trick considered a trick at all. In declamation after declamation, Gerardine and Maria stress the fact of their impending wedding and refer to the sacramental quality of their relationship. They intimate that their bond of love is so strong that their love-making is completely legitimate. The unborn child is not the result of carnality but a physical sign of the sanctity and spirituality of their contract. Thus the manner in which Middleton conceives this situation drives the two plots further apart instead of uniting them; no one in the low plot could think of regarding physical love as an extension of a spiritual relationship.

Plot disjunction is probably the play's main flaw. But other factors help make it singularly unsatisfactory. Lipsalve and Gudgeon maunder about the stage, laughed at first by one set of characters, then another. Their adventures, an incoherent mass of jests, are conceived so independently that they do not relate readily to the play as a whole. When the fop-gallants are center stage, what action there is grinds to a halt. Other roles are as ill-conceived: even Gerardine's position in the play is arbitrary. Too perfect for the play's good, the only character who knows what he wants and how to get it, Gerardine has no one to test or outwit him. Middleton may have meant to make Glister Gerardine's adversary, for early in the play the doctor promises to euchre Gerardine out of his possessions. But the scheme is not carried out. With no one actively opposing him, Maria's lover stands about, waiting for a sufficient number of tricks to be played, before he steps in and puts a stop to all the foolishness. As a result there is no spirit of competition, no tension between opposing forces, none of the game-like atmosphere good comedy can have.

The play's final scene is arbitrary in a number of ways, puzzling because the punishments do not fit the crimes.

Mistress Purge, who has furnished us with the most flagrant examples of promiscuity, is let off very lightly. Her misdeeds are exposed, but she is more or less acquitted when her husband fails to produce sufficient evidence against her. Meanwhile, Glister, whose evil actions are far fewer, has all his faults revealed, loses the guardianship of Maria, incurs the wrath of his wife, and is bilked of a thousand pounds by Gerardine. There is no apparent reason why the full weight of judgment should fall on him. Though he has been portrayed as an essentially negative character, few of his possibilities for evil have been realized. Had his plan to rob Gerardine been developed, losing the thousand pounds would have been an ironic reversal instead of gratuitous punishment. It is also disturbing that Lipsalve and Gudgeon, by contrast, escape judgment and correction entirely. Exhibited as fools at the beginning of the judgment scene— no more than they have been shown to be throughout the play—they are forgotten as the trial takes place.

Despite these faults, the play provokes some interest. Here Middleton takes his first steps toward an ironic confrontation with social ills and with evil itself. Gerardine and Maria do outwit a group of carnal characters who are oppressing them, and achieve victory with a fundamentally fleshy device, even if Middleton resists his own invention. Gerardine manages to turn the tables on the man who intended to cheat him, although the irony does not satisfy; Middleton is not sure how he wants the joke taken. He does not trust the audience to admit the essential justice in Gerardine's rather unusual course of action, arranging his marriage in the house of the man who forbade him to marry, stealing a dowry from the man who would not allow him one. Rather, he insists on the scheme's high moral purpose, against the evidence of human experience. His conception of noble character is such that Gerardine and Maria are simply too highminded to fit into the play world or to carry out the trick assigned them.

Since the latter parts of this study will dwell increasingly on the prevalence of irony in Middleton's comedy, it would be convenient to see his next play resolve the difficulties of *The Family*. Unfortunately it does not. In fact *The Phoenix* makes no advances in ironic technique at all. Exclusively a stage satire, it parades evils and follies before a disguised commentator throughout its course. The observer eventually emerges to punish wrongdoers and cleanse society of its evil tendencies.

Satiric process and form are more obvious here than they were in *The Family*. Middleton has separated romantic interest from satiric by making the commentator's assistant a principal in the play's slight love story. This frees the observer figure, Prince Phoenix, for full-time duty as commentator. Since he is a figure of political authority, a Prince, this presenter brings more moral weight to his role than did Gerardine.

That the setting is Italianate has little effect on the relevance of the satire.[4] Jacobean England thought Italians an especially villainous lot; consequently verse satire often clothed its villains and vices in Italianate names, though the vices and villains were demonstrably English. In keeping with the Italianate setting, *The Phoenix*'s story is more opera libretto than comic plot. It serves only to gather together a number of nearly independent scenes of villainy and foolery for observation and excoriation by Phoenix and his companion, Fidelio. A bevy of corrupt nobles persuade the elderly Duke of Ferrara to send his son Phoenix traveling, to add seasoning to his "time and virtue." The prince, knowing that the dukedom has fallen into corruption and decay in his father's declining years, never leaves home. He wanders through the city instead, inspecting the realm that

---

4. Italy was a common setting for plays of this form written in the years around the time of the ban on verse satire. See Marston's *The Fawn, Antonio and Mellida, Antonio's Revenge,* and *The Malcontent*; Jonson's original *Every Man in His Humour* and *Volpone*; Shakespeare's *Measure for Measure*.

will be his, finding corruption everywhere. The judge, Falso, is in league with highwaymen. Lawyer Tangle's tangled rhetoric exemplifies the knots of meaningless litigation in which the citizenry is caught. Aggressive and complacent lust are rampant; the Captain threatens the virtue of Fidelio's mother, and the Knight and the Jeweller's Wife are enjoying a much-too-cozy relationship. The ultimate villainy is a plot by the nobility to assassinate Phoenix and his father. After the Prince has discovered all, he reveals himself and brings the villains to justice, convicting the evil of sin and ascending to power after his father's abdication.

The Family's criticism dwelt mainly on lust and greed, vices that can be found in almost any social class. This play is more systematic in both approach and application. Phoenix, always the Prince, interests himself in vice as it affects his domain. In the broadest sense, the play is political; the inspection of vice and foolery is not solely comic but is given some semblance of social relevance. The play treats vice as found in characters who represent a number of different institutions and social classes. Phoenix uncovers abuses in Marriage (the Captain), Law (Tangle), Justice (Falso), the Court (Proditor), nobility (Lussurioso and Infesto), gentry (the Knight) and citizenry (the Jeweller's Wife).[5] An examination of the body politic, then: a metaphor particularly apt since the kingdom is full of hidden infection, discoverable only upon close examination. Phoenix is almost medical in defining his mission:

> To look into the heart and bowels of this dukedom, and, in disguise, mark all abuses ready for reformation or punishment.
> (I.i.100–102)

He performs his task with singleminded firmness. The tone here is much more unyielding than it was in *The Family*. Some of the harshness with which the Prince views evil

---

5. Alan C. Dessen, "Middleton's *The Phoenix* and the Allegorical Tradition," *SEL* 6 (1966):293.

may be due to the play's clarity of form; gratuitous tricks
do not distract one's attention. The protracted judgment
scene reflects the seriousness of attitude. Those whose maladies are not too advanced are pardoned and told to reform
themselves. Tangle is literally purged of his fault. But a
number of characters fare far more poorly. The would-be
seducers, the Captain and Proditor, are banished, as is the
Jeweller's Wife. Few of Middleton's plays refuse forgiveness to so many.

But the play is not simply negative. As the title indicates,
rejuvenation is as prominent a theme as punishment. Both
Prince and Dukedom go through a process of death and
then rebirth. Phoenix is obliterated for a time by disguise
and also suffers danger of death before entering a new and
fuller life. His city too is enlivened; his coming to power
signifies an end to corruption in Ferrara, where Phoenix is
now the force making possible such healthy and representa-
tive social changes as the marriage of Fidelio to the Niece.

Form is more meaningful here than it is in *The Family*.
There is a genuine attempt to connect the serious with the
grossly comic. The context of the jests lends them more
credibility. They are not designed only to be sat through
or worked around, but are objects of action. *The Family's*
jests proved no real threat to Gerardine; the vices of Ferrara are a serious problem for its future ruler. The political
scheme, then, gives Middleton a believable context in which
to register serious disapproval of vice.

Yet, even considering the relevance of form to material
and purpose, the play's structure does not seem fully satisfactory.[6] The play includes matter too widely divergent in
tone and type. Although it follows Northrop Frye's formula for a successful comedy, moving out of a period of
chaos and oppression toward a happy ending that calls
for our approval,[7] a reader does not leave the experience

---

6. But see Ellis-Fermor, p. 131.
7. *A Natural Perspective*, p. 167.

with the feelings one normally carries away from comedy. In fact one is not sure what to feel. Variety of action and character precludes a clear, unified response, especially since the overseer device does not relate the material effectively.

The comic response, of course, need not be simple; it is, in fact, ambivalent by nature. Satire, which this play tends to be, mixes the serious with the absurd. But Middleton forces his audience to respond in too many voices here. Fairly genial satire is mixed with bitter, serious and trivial objects are attacked with the same vehemence, and harsh satire sometimes spills over into straight melodrama, precluding a comic response entirely.

In the more serious portions of the play we confront not absurdity, however bitter, but unmitigated evil. Proditor, the lecherous, bloody courtier, is more responsible for this than any other character. There is nothing humorous about any of his major actions. He attempts to buy Fidelio's mother from her husband, the Captain, and plots the death of Phoenix and his father. As dark, secretive, and cynical as D'Amville in Tourneur's *The Atheist's Tragedy*, he is the same type of student of fate and the power of independent action.[8] Like D'Amville, Proditor has a consuming interest in the physical atmosphere that surrounds his crimes:

> *Proditor.* How is the air?
> *Phoenix.* O, full of trouble!
> *Proditor.* Does not the sky look piteously black?
> *Phoenix.* As if 'twere hung with rich men's consciences.
> *Proditor.* Ah, struck not a comet, like a carbunckle
> Upon the dreadful brow of twelve last night?
> *Phoenix.* Twelve? No, 'twas about one.
> *Proditor.* About one? most proper,
> For that's the duke.
>
> (V.i.8–15)

---

8. The names of Proditor's henchmen are Lussurioso and Infesto. Lussurioso is the name of a character in *The Revenger's Tragedy*, the Tourneur play sometimes ascribed to Middleton.

His loathsome conspiracies simply cannot be reconciled
with Falso's and Tangle's frivolous misdeeds. This is un-
fortunate, since the genial portions are the best parts of the
play. A lawyer as polysyllabic as the Marston figure in *The
Poetaster,* Tangle seems an early, more benign version of
Harry Dampit of *A Trick.* Tangle's discourses are quite
humorous, although they usually go on too long. The most
important scene of Falso, the corrupt justice, has much the
same type of humor, and a tone and texture we will see
more frequently in the ironic plays. Falso has a roguish,
knowing, yet strangely innocent attitude toward wrongdoing:

> I have been a youth myself: I ha' seen the day I could have told
> money out of other men's purses,—mass, so I can do now,—nor
> will I keep that fellow about me that dares not bid a man stand;
> for as long as drunkenness is a vice, stand is a virtue; but I would
> not have 'em taken. I remember now betimes in a morning, I
> would have peeped through the green boughs, and have had the
> prey presently, and then to ride away finely in fear: 'twas e'en
> venery to me, i' faith, the plesantest course of life! one would
> think every woodcock a constable and every owl an officer. But
> those days are past with me; and, a' my troth, I think I am a
> greater thief now, and in no danger. I can take my ease, sit in
> my chair, look in your faces now, and rob you; make you bring
> your money by authority, put off your hat, and thank me for
> robbing of you. O there is nothing to a thief under covert barn!
>   (III.i.59–75)

As excellent as they are, such scenes and sentiments lose
much of their effect because Middleton seems not to trust
himself here in creating so genial a character. He counter-
balances him with a group of characters so wicked that no
one would assent to their behavior, and the evil and hostility
of these thorough villains overpowers his geniality.

The unsatisfactory character of the *eiron* figure is another result of Middleton's efforts to impose on his materials a moral solution the work can not bear. Phoenix is
altogether contrived. Fidelio's chief function is to key our
response to the Prince's actions, and what he says always

far exceeds what Phoenix has actually achieved. He often
tells us how marvelous the Prince is, but we are never
shown that it is so. Like Maria and Gerardine, Phoenix is
portrayed as such a paragon of virtue that the effort to
integrate him into the action is doomed to failure.
Incompatibility of tone is not the play's only problem.
The judgment scene betrays the same inexplicable inequities
we saw in *The Family*. The treatment accorded the Jeweller's Wife, far harsher than that given her lover, seems
somewhat excessive. City gallants were proverbially short
of money and City wives typically suffered from the sexual
inadequacy of their business-obsessed husbands. The Knight
and Jeweller's Wife developed an effective reciprocal relationship. He was her "Pleasure," she his "Revenue." If
this put their love on a mercantile basis, it did not make a
great deal of difference to them. Nor does it concern Middleton too deeply until the judgment scene, where he treats
the Wife quite roughly. Phoenix feels that she and those
like her are responsible for all the ills of the time:

> Stand forth, thou one of those
> For whose close lusts the plague ne'er leaves the city,
> Thou worse than common! private, subtle harlot!
> That dost deceive three with one feigned lip,
> Thy husband, the world's eye, and the law's whip.
> Thy zeal is hot, for 'tis to lust and fraud,
> And dost not dread to make thy book thy bawd.
> Thou'rt curse enough to husband's ill-got gains,
> For whom the court rejects his gold maintains.
> (V.i.227–35)

Phoenix's target is the sin of lust itself; his indictment is
curious, though, for lust is not the salient factor in the
relationship of the Wife and the Knight. Their union
achieves comic force because of the matter-of-fact, commercial tone in which they deal with each other. For them sex
is a commodity. Like Marston, Middleton seems too preoccupied with the problem of sex and chastity to deal with

it forthrightly.[9] The same false note creeps into the banishment of the Captain, whose vice was also sexual. Middleton forces the issue by having the Captain self-consciously proclaim his villainy; after that, Phoenix exaggerates the thwarted danger:

> *Captain.* Well I'm yet glad I've liberty and these:
> The land has plagued me, and I'll plague the seas.
> *(Exit)*
> *Phoenix.* The scene is clear'd, the bane of brightness fled;
> Who sought the death of honour is struck dead.
> (II.ii.341–44)

This self-conscious moralizing contrasts markedly with the free-and-easy sentiments of Falso, probably the play's most notable creation. His forthright yet complacent attitude toward his own imperfection is the most memorable element of the work. Middleton again misjudges his material; he seeks to promote the least viable portions of it and to play down the qualities that could save the comedy.

Your Five Gallants employs the same attitude and dramatic structure and is plagued by the same problems. Like *The Family* and *The Phoenix,* it encloses comic actions within a serious frame story. It, too, has a serious, romantic, and essentially virtuous pair of lovers and a brace of scoundrels who must be detected, and corrected or punished. Its low plot employs the same tricks and scrapes, its high plot the same static, noble sentiments. The lover, Fitzgrave, plays the same part as Phoenix and Gerardine.

In another way, *Your Five Gallants* is a more paradoxical work. Although contemporary social ills are attacked more directly and clearly here than in the other plays, this is the most literary and conventional of the three. It contains more

---

9. See Samuel Schoenbaum, "The Precarious Balance of John Marston," *PMLA* 67 (1952) : 1069–78.

untransmuted jest book and pamphlet material than most Middleton plays. *The Family* and *The Phoenix* were built around one basic literary device. This play has two: it employs the presenter, of course, and couples with it the test-of-suitors motif, a device at least as old as the *Odyssey*.

Story line is again minimal. The hand of Katherine, a rich young virgin who has just completed a period of mourning for her father, is sought by the gentleman Fitzgrave and the gallants Frippery (a pawnbroker), Primero (a pimp), Goldstone (a sneak, thief, and cheat), Pursenet (a pickpocket), and Tailby (a whoremonger). The suitors agree to Katherine's request for a month's time in which to settle on one of them. Fitzgrave (the difference between him and the gallants is as bald as the difference between their names) decides to go into disguise as "some credulous scholar, easily infected with fashion, time and humour" (I.ii.93-94) to see why the gallants are hostile to him. As "Master Bouser" he discovers, in the course of the play, the specific vice of each of his rivals. In the inevitable judgment scene, the gallants' corruption is revealed in a masque designed by "Bouser," supposedly to grace Katherine's choosing of a husband. The social-climbing gallants are dismissed, and Katherine and Fitzgrave are united virtuously.

Commonplace as the pattern is, it does compare favorably, in some ways, with the dramatic schemes of the plays already examined. For the first time we are dealing with a fairly coherent social unit.

The body politic in *The Phoenix* did not provide enough definition. By contrast, *Your Five Gallants* deals with a group of characters ruled by the same interest. The play obtains form internally, shaped as it is by the ambitions of its characters. Six men desire the hand of the same woman; common concern allows for plausible plotting. Since the men are known to one another and engaged in the same endeavor, fortuitous circumstances need not connect their movements. The efforts of one of them to discover why the others are unworthy of the virgin's hand gives the play the chance for further unity, and its basic conflict.

This presents an agreeable opportunity. The actions of one gallant can be counterpointed against those of another until, after many expositions and recapitulations, observer and audience have witnessed a piece of folly almost musical in its resonances. Unfortunately that does not happen. Middleton does not take full advantage of his material. The tricks and plots of the five gallants are laid side by side, but Middleton makes little effort to connect them other than circumstantially. There is little ironic underplay; Middleton neglects a great opportunity for counterpoint in each gallant's ignorance of the character of the others. Late in the play, when the scoundrels do form an alliance, they only reveal their obtuseness in not having seen through one another earlier. Fitzgrave and the reader have done it easily long before.

In Middleton's more successful plays, the humor of the fool's role resides in his believing, up to the moment of recognition, in his own intelligence. The humor springing from his reversal stems not only from the fact of defeat but also from discrepancy between reality and his expectations. The fool has thought himself in the running for whatever the prize was or actually has had a chance at it. But here the five gallants are fools absolute, unworthy matches for Fitzgrave. As a result, the play is a much more static piece of work than it might be; discrete scenes forgo opportunities for connection.

A number of other faults serve to negate what is gained from the characters' having the same interests. *Your Five Gallants* has the by-now-familiar gap between levels of action. Katherine and Fitzgrave move on a much higher moral plane than the gallants. Gentlemen only in masquerade, they hide beneath fashionable attire a catalogue of vices that makes them totally unworthy of the rank they claim. All five are convicted of impudence (IV.v.74-89). Like Frippery, the pawnbroker, they have all risen meanly from the depths of society:

> For, having hardly raked five mark together, I rejoiced so in that small stock, which most providentially I ventured by water to Blackwall among fishwives; and in small time, what by weekly return and gainful restitution, it rize to a great body, beside a dish of fish for a present, that stately preserved me a seven-night.
> (I.i.299–305)

The vulgar tone of the passage is only part of a more serious consideration. The play notices from time to time that modern society seems generally peopled by characters of Frippery's stripe:

> Since impudence gains more respect than virtue,
> And coin than blood, which few can now deny,
> Who're your chief gallants then but such as I?
> (I.i.334–36)

However, the world is not in complete decline. There are still Katherine and Fitzgrave. Katherine is emphatically virginal throughout the play; were she cognizant of the gallants' venality she would recoil in horror from it. But there is no reason for her to do so; Middleton appraises her aptly by dropping her from the play between her setting a date for a decision and making it. She contributes little when she is on stage; Fitzgrave does all the work. A paragon of virtue, he fully controls the action, coolly observing the folly of the gallants and then quickly eliminating them from competition for Katherine's hand at the proper moment.

Katherine's absence and Fitzgrave's general quiescence weaken the play. If it were a factor in the action, the competition for Katherine would afford an opportunity for cohesion. But Katherine is absent from the thoughts of her suitors as well as from stage. The gallants, seemingly unconscious of the impending judgment, merely pursue their normal, witless activities. Fitzgrave sees only a series of disjointed vignettes, lifted bodily from the jest books.[10] The frame tale, then, contributes little to the play. The trial period is merely a time of waiting, especially in view of Fitzgrave's character. Katherine notices how admirable he is from the start of the play, so much so that we wonder why she needed to think things over at all.

The play is unusual in having two judgment scenes: a real one and a full dress rehearsal. The gallants expose themselves in all their faults in practice for and performance of Fitzgrave's masque. In their long, laborious, and pedantic unmasking, the gallants do not realize that the Latin they speak reveals their faults to Katherine. Middleton further stresses the seriousness of the gallants' vices by being lavish with punishments. Two of the villains are whipped and the others are forced to marry courtesans who will "loathe [them] worse than the foul'st disease" (V.ii.67). Unfortunately, the length of time spent on this dulls the memory of the more humorous portions of the play, the jest book tricks and gullings.

The same problem, then, plagues the three satiric plays: their essential humor is betrayed by their form and intent. That the plays are satires is hardly a consideration; the satire is lukewarm and general, almost barbless. *Your Five Gallants* does the most with a contemporary issue, centering its attack on social climbing, a problem current in the early years of James's reign. But even there the jests are too often untransmuted from their sources. In all the plays Middleton's targets are frequently so vague that we can only guess at what he is attacking. At best the satires do no more than register a sharp discontent with evil, a wish to drive it from the world.

---

10. *Your Five Gallants* is one of the richest mines in Middleton for source hunters. Since Middleton did so little to transmute the material, sources and analogues are readily identifiable.

A number of the "evil" characters—Falso, some of the gallants, and, to an extent, Mistress Purge—are often quite attractive, while the good are always cold, usually impossibly virtuous, and singularly undramatic. Middleton does not give the good their head, even after rigging the game for them in each of the plays. There is never a comic struggle testing the protagonist's will, wit, and humor—only series of set pieces depicting the low characters' depredations. Middleton's good people give us the impression that they can not function against their opponents at all. They are slow to ferret out evil, and when the low characters try to trick them, as they occasionally do, they succeed only too easily.

The hidden observer's presence has a harmful effect on the movement, tone, and spirit of the plays; at once standard and arbiter, he does not readily fit into comic action. Basically an expositor, he must be true to his nature, offspring as he is of the verse satirist *persona*. As the central figure in each play, he causes them to commit one of the cardinal sins of drama, to tell rather than show.

Despite these flaws, Middleton's early drama is not completely meretricious. If it is not clear what evils Middleton is attacking, if the judgment scenes are confused, it is still obvious that he is concerned with social conduct. He is interested in how people cooperate with and use one another in situations on almost every level of personal relations. He suggests, at times with wry humor, that society and the world are in general decay. In *Your Five Gallants* Pursenet talks of a woman he thought his own:

> Well, what a horrible age do we live in, that a man cannot have a quean to himself! let him but turn his back, the best of her is chipt away like a court loaf, that when a man comes himself, has nothing but bumbast; and these are two simple chippings here. Does my boy pick and I steal to enrich myself, to keep her, to maintain him? why, this is right the sequence of the world. A lord maintains her, she maintains a knight, he maintains a whore, she maintains a captain. So in like manner the pocket keeps my

boy, he keeps me, I keep her, she keeps him; it runs like quick-silver from one to another.

(III.ii.96–107)

Things are such that a man cannot be sure of his own whore; corruption confounds itself.

Middleton was not prepared, while writing these plays, to show his audience a world of nearly unmitigated evil. He would not take a full look at the worst for years—until the time of *Women, Beware Women* and *The Changeling.* Here he insists there are a type of person and kind of society that remain unsullied. He attempts to picture the triumph of virtue and duly pushes his characters through to victory. But his successes do not satisfy his readers, who would like to see victor less and vanquished more. We cannot help feeling that characters so vital and potentially humorous do not deserve the treatment they finally receive. Middleton seems not to have been pleased, either, as the plays we now turn to show.

In the next several chapters we shall see what Middleton did in his major comedies to allow his rogues room to breathe and play, and to let his audience laugh more easily. He found a way of achieving this without giving up the attempt to espouse a theory of social morality. As he developed a sense of proportion, an ability to match crime and punishment and to forgive where forgiveness is possible, he discovered he could write very humorous, lighthearted plays that still take a stand on social ills, indicate desirable and undesirable ways to live, and put their case clearly. He devised characters who could operate effectively in the corrupt world and yet maintain an essential honesty. In doing so he revised his own notions of moral conduct, although his confusion does not wholly disappear until *Chaste Maid.*

How he came to deal with a problematic world maturely will be my central concern in examining *A Trick, Mad World, Chaste Maid,* and first of all, *Michaelmas Term.*

3

Michaelmas Term

*M*ICHAELMAS *Term* serves as a convenient link
between the satirical plays and the other City
Comedies. It clearly contains elements of both styles. Like
the satires its tone is sometimes harsh. In places its attitude
toward evil is stern and unyielding, and it makes some use
of the hidden commentator. But in accomplishment, form,
and even tone, *Michaelmas Term* is closer to *A Trick,* for
instance, than to the satires. The presenter does not dominate the play; the tonal split, though still a factor, is not
an overwhelming concern. Didacticism no longer obliterates
action. Instead, a multiple plot runs its course, themes counterpointing one another ironically. The play has movement;
and Middleton's directing of the action is, for once, fairly
subtle.

Like the other mature plays, *Michaelmas Term* is far
more lifelike, quite literally, than the satiric comedies, which
themselves give little support to the notion of Middleton
as realist. As we have seen, their form is artificial and quite

static, their basic pattern of action borrowed from a literary source, verse satire. The local references are generally insignificant and intermittent, merely hooks from which to hang jokes and commonplace stage devices. Specific attack on contemporary social ills is not a major factor. Instead, we see the low humor of characters who could wear the livery of almost any occupation or belong to any social class and who have strongly literary blood lines.

Compared to these plays, *Michaelmas Term* is "realistic," even though its two plots are a mixture of the contemporary and the conventional.[1] In the main story, Richard Easy, just fallen heir to the family estate in Essex, comes up to London to see the town. On arrival he falls in with a group of scoundrels, among whom are Shortyard and Falselight, two "spirits" of the woolen draper Quomodo, who covets Easy's land. Shortyard, disguised as a gallant named "Blastfield," introduces Easy to the City ritual of gaming, whoring, and carousing and persuades him to cosign a note held by Quomodo. "Blastfield" defaults, and Shortyard—first as bailiff, then as alderman—helps Quomodo take possession of the collateral, the Essex estate. But Quomodo, drunk with triumph, inexplicably thinks his family will not respond to his death with the proper gratitude and concern. He pretends to die, and goes about in disguise watching his worst fears come true.[2] Shortyard cheats his son, Sim Quomodo, out of the property; Sim voices his contempt for his father; the merchant's daughter, Susan, marries a man he had not favored; and his wife Thomasine, far from dissolving in grief, remarries immediately—and the groom is Easy. Quomodo discovers himself, but not before foolishly signing away his rights to Easy's property. He recovers his wife and goods but sees himself defeated on all other fronts.

The underplot parallels this story in form and content

---

1. One of the first to notice this was Knights, p. 258.
2. See Massinger's *City Madam*, Chapman's *All Fools*, Jonson's *Volpone*, and Steele's *The Funeral* for the same motif.

and is at points connected to it. Andrew Lethe (*né* Gruel) aspires to gentility as Quomodo does, but he starts his ascent a few rungs further down the ladder. Quomodo aspires to Easy's land, Lethe to Quomodo's daughter. Lethe also affects gallantry, and this brings him down. In mistaken emulation of his betters, he keeps a whore, a lowly country wench who is also a social climber. He is defeated largely because Rearage, the "true gentleman" Susan eventually marries, tells her of his libertinage.

The play deals, then, with what appear to be contemporary Jacobean types and problems: grasping merchants, debt-ridden gentry, social climbers, struggles over land and inheritances. It does have a patina of realism, for which the setting is largely responsible. Most of the action takes place in the street. The street is the traditional setting of Plautine and Terentian comedy, but Middleton attempts to place this one firmly in London. Easy, Shortyard, Quomodo, and the gallants go through their paces before merchant's booth and ordinary, and even in Paul's. There is also an attempt at temporal location. The play deals with London during the chief legal term, when litigants streamed into town. Set in such a time, the play deals with the immigration into the City of no less than five characters. The local and temporal frame gives the stories a plausibility and solidity a more purely literary background might not have offered.

Yet the time reference is hardly substantial. Middleton discounts it in the Induction, as we shall see in a moment. And after Rearage and Salewood's opening dialogue (I.i.1–39), there are only two passing references to Term time in the rest of the play. Granted, a Judge appears in the last scene, dispenses punishment, and has the play's last words. But one can argue that the Judge is the character Michaelmas Term, returned in costume to complete the frame motif begun in the Induction.[3]

---

3. An element of the play largely overlooked in the criticism. Ruby Chatterji says of the Induction, "Though excellent satire by itself, it bears

This device, far more conventional than mimetic, further distances the action from surface reality. Its chief function is not informational. It does not localize the play so much as it introduces its themes and helps unite the two plots. Each action and configuration of character in the Induction prefigures significant actions and groupings in the play itself. The Induction's players are Michaelmas Term personified, his page, and the three lesser legal terms. The master-page relationship suggests later pairings: Quomodo and his page, "Blastfield" and Easy, Lethe and the pimp Hellgill, and even Quomodo and Easy. The relationship of Michaelmas Term to the other terms recurs in the groupings of Quomodo and his spirits, and then of Easy and Rearage, Salewood, and Cockstone, the gallants who introduce him to London ways.

Michaelmas Term opens the Induction "new come up out of the country," exchanging his "whitish" country cloak, in a piece of obvious symbolism, for the black robe appropriate to law court and City. When he asks the page how many come up to the courts, the boy's answer surprises him:

> *Michaelmas Term.* Come they up thick enough?
> *Boy.* Oh, like hops and harlots, sir.
> *Michaelmas Term.* Why dost thou couple them?
> *Boy.* Oh, very aptly, for as the hop well boiled will make a man not stand upon his legs, so the harlot in time will leave a man no legs to stand upon.
> *Michaelmas Term.* Such another, and be my heir! I have no child, Yet have I wealth would redeem beggary.
>
> (Inductio, 13–20)[4]

The three lesser terms enter in dumb show, leading in a poor fellow whom they give "rich apparel, a page, and a

---

no structural relationship to the play and could easily be cut in a production." "Unity and Disparity in *Michaelmas Term,*" *SEL* 8 (1968):352. Barker ignores the Induction entirely.

4. The Regents Renaissance Drama edition, ed. Richard Levin (Lincoln, Neb., 1966), is cited throughout the chapter.

pander." The terms plead with Michaelmas Term for favors, which he promises to grant. With that, the Induction has prefigured the basic actions of the play: migration from country to City; change of country garments (and the attitudes that clothing signifies) for gaudy, more worldly apparel; struggles over inheritances, money, and women; attempts to scale the social ladder; and unexpectedly good answers to apparent problems.

Within this conventional frame, which gives us a set for viewing what follows, Middleton uses literary material to dramatize the action. Quomodo tricks Easy with devices detailed in Greene's coney-catching pamphlets and other literary sources.[5] The characters' conduct is often proverbial. Thomasine, for instance, is not only a curious wife (II.iii), but also remarries with a haste characteristic of widows in tales and jests dating back to Chaucer's time. The play also makes use of patterns basic to Roman comedy. *Michaelmas Term* has an excitable old man (Quomodo) who blocks the path of a rather silly young one (Easy); a woman (Susan Quomodo) pursued by a suitor (Rearage) who eventually wins her; scapegoats (Shortyard and Falselight) banished at the end of the play; and a young woman (the Country Wench) whose father comes to town to rescue her. Middleton employs these character types and the strategies in which they involve themselves throughout the ironic plays just as he had used them, generally in embryo, in the satires. Though the protagonists of the satiric plays are far from humorous, they usually do find their paths blocked by older or more experienced characters.

---

5. For possible sources and analogues see Mildred Gaylor Christian, "Non-Dramatic Sources for the Rogues in Middleton's Plays" (Diss., Chicago, 1932), pp. 54–59; R. C. Bald, "The Sources of Middleton's City Comedies," *JEGP* 33 (1934):373–87; Margery Fisher, "Notes on the Sources of Some Incidents in Middleton's London Plays," *RES* 15 (1939):284; David George, "Thomas Middleton's Sources: A Survey," *N.&Q.*, n.s. 18 (1971):19.

A fixture of Attic comedy already used in *The Phoenix,*
the death-rebirth cycle, occurs here on at least three levels.
Most obviously, Quomodo dies and is reborn, and the special twist given his "death" provides much of the play's
humor. He finds his position clarified but trades blissful
ignorance for a new life in which he will be his "own afflic-
tion" (V.iii.164). Easy experiences death and rebirth in
another sense. He becomes a nonperson in the world of
gallantry once he has lost the estate that guaranteed him
both livelihood and status. After realizing his errors, he is
reborn, elevated again to the rank of independent landowner with the help of Thomasine and blind luck. On yet
another level, Andrew Gruel, the son of an "honest upright
tooth drawer," dies to the world to reemerge as Andrew
Lethe, a gallant who cannot remember other gallants'
names. In the judgment scene the Lethe *persona* is destroyed
when his mother recognizes Gruel and repudiates him.

The keynotes of the judgment scene—recognition, knowledge of self, repudiation—round off a theme introduced in
the very early moments of the play. The Induction's last
lines, Michaelmas Term's address to the audience, indicate
how actions, actors, and even audience are to be measured:

> Why call we this play by such a dear and chargeable title, *Michael-*
> *mas Term*? Know it consents happily to our purpose, though
> perhaps faintly to the interpretation of many, for he that expects
> any great quarrels in law to be handled here will be fondly de-
> ceived; this only presents those familiar accidents which happen'd
> in town in the circumference of those six weeks whereof Michael-
> mas Term is lord. *Sat sapienti;* I hope there's no fools i' th' house.
>   (Inductio, 66–75)

The play's complex game is played in terms of levels of
knowledge—both knowledge possessed at play's start and
knowledge gained in its course. Here knowledge means the
ability to see what words and titles, the clothing of idea
and action, really signify. Just as the audience (and critics

too) might be fooled by the title, so those characters who mistake appearance for reality will be deceived. *Michaelmas Term* ultimately deals with the wise and the foolish—those who can cope with the City world, regardless of appearances, and those who cannot.

As the Induction intimates, with its emphasis on changes in locale, clothing, social position, and wisdom, the process of initiation is at the heart of the play. On a fundamental level it introduces neophytes into a world more complex, sophisticated, and difficult than the one they had previously known. In the City they either learn or fail to learn what they must know about themselves and the world in order to live effectively. Easy is the primary initiate, and does rather well: for a time this newcomer even displaces the arch-cozener Quomodo, taking over his home, possessions, and wife. When we see Easy in Quomodo's place, we realize that he is equipped, for the first time, to function in a world of men.

The rite of initiation is often celebrated ceremoniously. Here the new apprehension of themselves that characters attain and the changes that lead to self-awareness are often related to a change in garments, a frequent component of ritual. Lethe dons the clothing of a City gallant and pretends to be one; but this only makes him the butt of jokes from real gallants. He is more successful in having his pimp seduce the Country Wench with the promise of City finery. Quomodo, too, knows the value of fashion. His man Shortyard, disguised as a gallant, snares Easy, who at first is far too willing to play the role of heedless gallant.

But Lethe's and Quomodo's triumphs are temporary, for both look only to the surface of things. Lethe cannot see past the flashy clothes of his mistress to the coarse and all-too-willing girl beneath. He mistakes a whore for a "gentlewoman of a great house, noble parentage, unmatchable education" (III.i.73-74), and this leads to his downfall. Similarly, Quomodo does not see the real Easy beneath the foppish exterior and misjudges his capacity to learn. Short-yard judges the young man more accurately:

> But for Easy,
> Only good confidence did make him foolish,
> And not lack of sense, that was not it;
> 'Tis worldly craft beats down a scholar's wit.
> (IV.iii.14–17)

But Quomodo, swollen with success, teaches Easy how to regard bonds and contracts and how much to trust people, lessons Easy comes to understand and use.

Quomodo and Lethe suffer similar punishments for their ignorance. In the judgment scene, before Easy, the Country Wench, and all the other characters, both are made to shed appearance and finally realize what they are. Mother Gruel shows her son what City life has done to him, as the changed-clothing theme is picked up again:

> How art thou chang'd!
> Is this suit fit for thee, a tooth-drawer's son?
> This country has e'en spoil'd thee since thou
>   cam'st hither;
> Thy manners . . . better than thy clothes,
> But now whole clothes, and ragged manners.
> It may well be said that truth goes naked,
> For when thou hadst scarce a shirt, thou hadst
> More truth about thee.
> (V.iii.156–63)

Quomodo, after stripping off his disguise, admits that he is "the man that liv'd the famous coz'ner" (V.iii.21). The bailiff he was saw all too well that his family and household knew him for the scoundrel he is.

The ability to look below the surface, to engage reality, is the measure of the characters' success. The survivors do not mistake fine clothing for true gentility, or the word of a stranger dressed as a gallant for truth. These are not always easy lessons to learn. The City in *Michaelmas Term* is a bewildering maze of disguise and intrigue. The play world is full of rapacious characters who are all too willing to profit at the expense of others. But even in the midst of corruption those who are flexible profit most. The Country Wench's father takes a steadfast stand against the City, inveighing against it in didactic, jog-trot couplets:

> Oh, heavens, I know the price of ill too well,
> What the confusions are, in whom they dwell,
> And how soon maids are to their ruins won;
> One minute, and eternally undone. . . .
>
> (II.ii.27–30)

But his moralism does him little good. The least successful and discerning character in the play, he does not even recognize his daughter when he sees her in her City clothes.

Rearage and Easy are more successful because they ultimately are not fooled by surfaces as the Wench's father is. Easy watches Quomodo the bailiff sign away his rights to the estate; Rearage sees through Lethe from the start. But in looking beyond appearance, neither ignores the City's substance. The play's London is not to be rejected entirely. The young men learn the ways of Mammon, too, while still acting with concern for others and with a sense of honor in a world of conflicting rights and obligations.

When Thomasine first shows an interest in Easy, he does not repulse her; he is happy to take money from her even before Quomodo's disappearance. But their sexual relationship begins only after Quomodo's "death." Faithful in deed if not in spirit, Thomasine states only then that "I have the leisure now both to do that gentleman good and do myself a little pleasure" (IV.iii.40–41). And when Quomodo rises from the dead, she returns to him, however

reluctantly.[6] Her concern for herself and for Easy is revealing. Their match is more satisfactory than her union
with Quomodo, a marriage in name only. The merchant
had apparently neglected her domestically and sexually. He
showed her little regard; she complained that he was "no
man." By contrast she and Easy have an honest, affection-
ate, reciprocal partnership, as did the Knight and Jeweller's
Wife in *The Phoenix*. She gives Easy aid and solace; he
gives her what Quomodo apparently could not.

In Middleton, wives' unfaithfulness generally has a very
specific basis: older husbands' not fulfilling their part of
the marriage contract. In the mature comedies, Middleton
champions and arranges relationships in which neither party
gives more than he receives. He tries to put society on a
basis of mutuality, creating a world in which love and creature comforts ameliorate the condition of both parties.

The satirical plays' treatment of love and sexuality is
unsatisfactory. They portray only two types of relationships:
thoroughly corrupt and incredibly pure ones. Here Middleton is able to deal with the theme in a more human, balanced, compassionate way. The new ease is reflected in
style in the fact that Rearage does not even use stilted
verse in his pursuit of Susan, a courtship that combines
ideal and realistic considerations.

Rearage wins her because he bases his suit upon his love
for her, while the impostor, Lethe, has his eye only on her
"happy portion" of 700 pounds. (III.i.203-6). The real
gallant also teaches her to distinguish between true and
false:

> Pardon my willful blindness, and enjoy me;
> For now the difference appears too plain
> Betwixt a base slave and a true gentleman.
> (V.ii.8–10)

---

6. Even though critical opinion often holds that she does not. See Bullen,
1:xxviii; Gibbons, p. 131; Barker, p. 50; Dunkel, p. 25; for the correct
interpretation, see Thomas Middleton, *Plays,* ed. Martin Sampson (New
York, 1915), p. 16; Levin ed., p. 127n. See my "Remarriage in *Michaelmas
Term,*" *N.&Q.,* n.s. 19 (1972):460-61.

But even Rearage does not scorn the dowry, though romantic considerations compel him more. Middleton's more laudable characters can be practical people; honest actions can, after all, have pleasant worldly results.

The ability to distinguish substance from accidents and to act both for oneself and for others out of a complex of motives reflects a certain maturity. Initiation is a recognition of growth into adulthood, and one of the play's basic concerns is the opposition of parent and maturing child. In several cases a parent's desires or beliefs affect the child's movement in society. The most significant relationships involve Lethe and his mother, the Country Wench and her father, Sim and Quomodo, and, of course, Quomodo and Easy.

Quomodo, who had been trying to assume Easy's role as heir, unwittingly takes the part of father to him. After he has bilked him of his lands, Quomodo thinks he can afford to give the boy parental advice. Waxing poetic, he quotes Easy verse:

> "Make this account, come better days or worse,
> So many bonds abroad, so many boys at nurse."
> (III.iv.150–51)

Like Quomodo's bonds, Easy has been "at nurse," a mere babe in the woods at the hands of Quomodo and his spirits. But Quomodo does not realize that growth results from being at nurse. Like the broken bonds Quomodo mentions, Easy, a broken man grown strong, will "leap in his face." Quomodo's advice, though clever, is not clever enough. Quomodo feels one must break children, not bonds. The child he has broken here will come back to break him, precisely because he has gone to school on Quomodo's advice: "Say you so, sir?" says Easy, "I'll think upon your counsel hereafter for't" (III.iv.145). The Quomodo-Easy

relationship has resonances in the other character confiura-
tions. Easy pays close attention to Quomodo and finally
triumphs. The other young people reject their parents more
or less consciously and encounter difficulties. The Wench,
Lethe, and Sim Quomodo learn nothing from their elders
and also find that they are used by characters more experienced in the ways of the City. Lethe is fooled by Rearage,
the Wench is corrupted by Lethe, and Sim is cheated out
of his inheritance by Shortyard.

Another action parallels these, though it is in some ways
their reverse. With the help of Thomasine and abundant
good luck, a grown-up Easy trips the suddenly childish
Quomodo, who loses the Essex estate he had worked so
hard to get. The two major cozenings, Quomodo's of Easy
and Easy's of Quomodo, parallel each other on several
levels, though they differ in motivation, development, and
detail. The two characters are most alike in their initiation
into new and greater knowledge. After teaching Easy his
lessons, Quomodo finds that he has something to learn
himself. The gusto and surety apparent in his attack show
us a man of confirmed ability, and the ease with which he
gulls Easy engenders overconfidence. His shrewdness plays
him false, for he tries to go too far. He falls prey to his
own penetrating understanding of the life process:

> And because I see before mine eyes that most of our heirs prove
> notorious rioters after our deaths, and that cozenage in the father
> wheels about to folly in the son, our posterity commonly foil'd
> at the same weapon at which we play'd rarely, and being the
> world's beaten word, what's got over the devil's back (that's by
> knavery) must be spent under his belly (that's by lechery) ; being
> awake in these knowings, why should not I oppose 'em now, and
> break destiny of her custom, preventing that by policy, which
> without it must needs be destiny?
>
> (IV.i.81–91)

Although Quomodo realizes that heirs sometimes take land
and money less seriously than their fathers do, he is still

surprised when he sees the theory apply to himself. Blinded by pride and his own aspirations to scholarship, he cannot see his son's simplicity.

Shortyard, who understood Easy's basic intelligence, also sees what is wrong with Quomodo. Ironically, he voices his opinion in Quomodo's presence, disguised as an Alderman:

> We have neither posterity in town, nor hope for any abroad; we have wives, but the marks have been out of their mouths these twenty years, and, as it appears, they did little good when they were in. We could not stand about it, sir; to get riches and children too, 'tis more than one man can do.
>
> (IV.i.30–34)

The old man refuses to recognize himself in the situation. He overestimates his own powers. Though he refuses to see it, Quomodo, for all his experience and ecstatic day-dreams of copulation, proves himself an ineffectual figure on the verge of replacement. He possesses money, a wife, a son, and land and cannot deal adequately with any of them. He fails to realize that he will lose his goods when he disappears, and that he cannot satisfy his wife, does not realize his son's imbecility, and would misuse the land.

Easy is energetic, potent, and shows a capacity for growth. Once educated he will be able to make better use of things than Quomodo, and the play works toward giving them to him. If society is to be viable, it must be controlled by men who can produce children and train them properly, can husband the land, using yet conserving it. Life-oriented comedy, then, drives toward overthrow of the old man. The young man is first educated, then presented a bride, or wealth, or both. Although Easy does not obtain a bride (Rearage, the other oppressed young gallant, does), he gets his lands back. Quomodo had been a genuine threat to the estate. The old merchant has a vision of fertility, in which he and his citizen friends on their way to the country will "laugh, and lie down, get all our wives with child against a bank" (IV.i.76-77), but we know he cannot fulfill it. His plans for the estate's trees are revealing:

> A little thing, three hundred pound a year,
> Suffices nature, keeps life and soul together!
> I'll have 'em lop'd immediately; I long
> To warm myself by th' wood.
>
> (IV.i.66-69)

Quomodo is not willing to cultivate the land, to make it more fertile. Instead, he plans to use the life on it to furnish the warmth his own worn-out body cannot provide.

Easy represents the force inheriting what Quomodo cannot sustain. For a time, Easy even possesses the still-vital wife of the old man. The process echoes ancient fertility rituals, as Quomodo, the old king of City cozenage, dies for a time and is immediately replaced by a new man. Continuity is suggested even in the vices from which the chief characters suffer. Easy fails because he has experienced nothing; Quomodo because he has experienced everything. Quomodo tries to break out of the cycle; by pretending death, he attempts to conquer it, to master the future. Of course he loses this battle.

The unmasking of Quomodo and Lethe, and the rehabilitation of Easy come with a rush, but there is a feeling of rightness about the way things stand at play's end. Nature itself seems to assent to the completed process:

> *Easy.* No, my good lord, the lands know the right heir;
> I am their master once more.
>
> (V.iii.76-77)

Here, Easy, who had to have everything explained to him when he first came to the City, explains things to the Judge. Quomodo, who plotted in secret, is exposed to the world, utterly without resources. The man with the perfect scheme can no longer even lie with his wife in "perfect memory."

We sense that the process will continue. It is possible to foresee Easy's growing old and foolish, being supplanted by another young man. The comic world has been brought at the end of the play only to a point of balance. No one has reached perfection, but all have had their position in life and in the comic world clarified. If all are imperfect— Easy slow to learn, Quomodo reluctant to relinquish power, Lethe and the Wench too willing to accept surface values— almost all are forgiven. Here Middleton accepts the fact that man is a fallen creature in a fallen world. Only Short- yard and Falselight are banished from the play world, and there is little real punishment. The playwright pardons most of his characters, who bear away from the judgment scene not stripes but increased self-knowledge and clarified understanding. They are released on the recognizance of their own foolishness and imperfection. If the harshness of a comedy can be measured by the amount and type of pun- ishment meted out in the judgment scene,[7] *Michaelmas Term* stands at an intermediate position between the satirical plays and more "genial" works such as *Mad World* and *A Trick*. Almost everyone here has been settled or resettled into society. Easy has reached man's estate, regaining his Essex lands; Rearage and Lethe, who has married the Country Wench, have each taken brides suitable to their merits; Quomodo has been deprived of his evil "spirits" and has a clearer idea of his relationship with his wife and son.

Analyses that criticize Middleton for "amorality" miss the point.[8] Retribution is impressively fair in this work and is meted out quite accurately. Those who take unfair ad- vantage are put at disadvantage. Those not responsible for their downfall are effortlessly restored to their former posi- tions. Cheaters are cheated, and those who use their wits craftily see craft rebound against them.

7. See Frye, *The Anatomy of Criticism*, pp. 43–48.
8. Barker, pp. 85–86.

And all this has been accomplished with a good deal of wit and humor. Middleton is not the complete didacticist some think him to be. The nature of the form here makes for a grace and charm noticeably absent in the satires. With plot, subplot, and minor vignettes counterpointing one another, there is no longer so much dependence on a cumbersome frame story. *Michaelmas Term* shows the breakneck speed and insouciance characteristic of Middleton's funniest work. His prose is flexible and supple, less slangy than the rogue pamphlets' but just as vigorous and delightfully casual. Even the verse, so deadly before, can be comic, especially when Quomodo delivers his cynical, deadly accurate aphorisms. This is the first play this study has encountered in which characters are not cardboard figures, but change and grow. Quomodo, selfish, rapacious, and cunning, is still not a Volpone. His ecstasies always have a genial touch:

> Oh, that sweet, neat, comely, proper, delicate parcel of land, like a fine gentlewoman i' th' waist, not so great as pretty, pretty; the trees in summer whistling, the silver waters by the banks harmoniously gliding. I should have been a scholar; an excellent place for a student, fit for my son that lately commenc'd at Cambridge, whom now I have plac'd at Inns of Court.
>
> (II.iii.82–88)

The play's irony is the main contributor to its humor. Muriel Bradbook has said that Middletonian irony depends more on dramatic situation than language.[9] It would be more accurate to say that his irony works on several levels, including the verbal. As lowly a device as *double-entendre* depends entirely on the duality of words, and Middleton's comedy is dual there as well as on much more exalted levels.

A major ironic achievement of *Michaelmas Term* is its characterization. The play concerns itself with the unprincipled social climbing of dentists' sons, and with the frittering away of ancient estates, but the basic conflict here, as

---

9. Bradbrook, p. 155.

elsewhere in Middletonian comedy, does not fall along class lines. Middleton's mature dramaturgy has complex sympathies. Characters may be recognizable as gentry or merchants but neither class has a monopoly on cunning, intelligence, or the reader's admiration and sympathy. If Middleton was writing, as some theorize, for an upper-class audience, they must have been dissatisfied with their surrogate figure, Easy. It is difficult to summon much sympathy for him in the first two-thirds of the play. The young heir is so gullible that he almost requires the treatment Quomodo gives him. Such a booby would not know what to do with his land if he could retain it. At that, he is treated rather gently; the play's other gallants evoke much less sympathy. Rearage and his cronies, Salewood and Cockstone, at times seem somewhat unsavory. Though the idea is not fully developed, Middleton casts them as indigent gallants who gouge their country tenants and fleece unsuspecting innocents much as Quomodo cheats Easy (II.i.165-72).[10] However, Middleton did not quite resolve their position. Though they are viewed unfavorably from time to time, they also occasionally serve as commentators. Then their role parallels that of the *eiron* of the earlier plays, though the part is much reduced.[11] In fact there is only one significant passage of semi-Juvenalian railing in the play (I.i.185-95). Notions of true gallantry are usually not preached to us; we draw our own conclusions by contrasting the conduct of Rearage and Lethe and by evaluating their success and failure.

Occasionally we see gallants from the merchants' point of

10. The dissolute, ruined gallant who preys on others of his own stripe is a recurrent figure in the pamphlets. See, for example, Middleton's *Father Hubbard's Tale,* esp. "The Ant's Tale."

11. Rearage and Salewood (and Thomasine and the Father) are the main hidden observers. The latter two tend to be superfluous in that role. Examination of the gallants' scenes as observers (see II.iii; III.i.269-71; III.iv. 242-47) shows that they do not advance the action at all but only offer moralizing that the weight of the play could have carried without their comments.

view, especially in Shortyard's and Falselight's commentary. Disguised as aldermen, they discuss the perils of trusting their "betters." What they say has substance; for their comments, though ironic, spring from Easy's real failure to pay his bills:

> *Shortyard.* Gentlemen! 'Slid, they were born to undo us, I think; but, for my part, I'll make an oath before Master Quomodo here, ne'er to do gentlemen good while I live.
> *Falselight.* I'll not be long behind you.
>
> (IV.i.8–11)

The statement is a little unfair, since Easy is much the more aggrieved party, but the fact of his legal obligation remains. Like young gentlemen throughout Middleton's comedy, he shows an irresponsibility that he himself will eventually recognize as harmful.

If the gallants are not perfectly good, the merchant class of the play is not completely evil. Easy receives valuable assistance from Thomasine, who possesses discernment as well as conscience. She realizes that true gentility is superior to Lethe's ridiculous, vulgar posturing and opposes his suit for her daughter. Of course Quomodo, whose every desire is vulgar, including his wish to become a landed proprietor, is blinded by Lethe's flash and show. The most memorable character in the play, Quomodo best exemplifies Middleton's ability to achieve comic balance. He is a villain, but a truly comic one who takes such delight in his craft that we cannot seriously consider him an evil force.

Irony also functions in the characters' attitudes toward themselves. They are generally closest to a fall when they feel themselves at the height of their powers. Exulting in the excellence of his death scheme, Quomodo asks, "But am I not a wise fool now?" (IV.iv.4). The answer comes about fifteen lines later, when his whole world begins to fall around him. His prediction of his own downfall, though unconscious, lightens the humor; several characters blind

to realities obvious to everyone else betray the same for-
givable, all-too-human vulnerability. The gulling of Easy
is the more humorous because he thinks himself shrewd
and yet consistently falls for such old, conventional tricks.
Quomodo is victim again in failing to see the resemblance
between Sim and the innocent Easy, though it shouts for
recognition. Lethe does not see his own tawdriness; his
idea that women will inevitably love him is patently absurd.

Ironic plotting and characterization inform a larger
vision, more complex, ironic, and ambiguous. The world of
Michaelmas Term is neither totally negative nor totally
positive. Though craft and trickery are defeated at last, it
takes craft and trickery to do it. The London of the play is
a living, growing, changing organism, but one with diseased
parts. Greed, lust, and self-interest function in every walk
of life.

Here triumph and failure are not functions of such an
arbitrary factor as social background. To succeed, a character must realize the City's complexity and fallenness and
act upon his knowledge. The successful use their knowledge
well—for their own benefit and for the good of those who
do not misuse them. Even then, when they achieve knowledge of good and evil and take the better part, one is not
sure the choice is permanent. When Susan confesses to
Rearage that she was wrong—and foolish—to prefer Lethe,
he accepts her apology but knows how transitory such a
mood can be:

> I do embrace thee in the best of love.—
> (*Aside.*) How soon affections fail, how soon they prove!
> (V.ii.11–12)

Although the play is a real achievement, it is far from
perfect. Despite all the correspondences, there is an impatience with vice in Lethe's story curiously out of keeping
with the tone of the main plot. The main story itself tends
to fall into two parts, separated by Quomodo's death. Easy,

though he acts with self-assurance, confidence, and competence as Thomasine's husband, must finally depend on Quomodo to fool himself. There is also something out of tune about Thomasine's return to Quomodo and the harsh cynicism of the gallants. Finally, the play lacks the fascinating interplay of conflicting drives and emotions that we find in some Middleton plays, *A Trick,* for instance.

But these are minor flaws in what is for the most part an effective work. In general *Michaelmas Term* gives us a well-paced, coherent picture of a complex, ironic world. Susanne Langer confirms Middleton's artistic intuition: the comic resides not in individual incidents but in the placing of those incidents in larger, more universal patterns.[12] *Michaelmas Term* presents a more positive picture than is often assumed. It uses conventional situations and patterns of action, under a patina of realism, to convince us that the struggle between young and old, the process of maturing and socializing oneself, is a never-ending and perpetually amusing one. In the play we are about to study, the achievement is even greater.

---

12. Langer, p. 347.

4

A Trick to Catch the Old One

A Trick has a high critical reputation. Some of the luster is doubtless reflected glow from Massinger's *A New Way to Pay Old Debts,* a play modeled on it and praised greatly by L. C. Knights.[1] But Middleton's is a very solid work and deserves the good things said about it, for whatever reason. The play has been dated only approximately; though internal analysis is not an infallible tool for dating Jacobean plays, *A Trick* does show a more advanced grasp of technique than *Michaelmas Term* (as does *Mad World*). In most ways, the plotting is more satisfactory here than in *Michaelmas Term.* The point of attack has been pushed beyond the young man's loss of his patrimony, and the whole play is given over to his scheming his recovery. *Michaelmas Term* dealt with that most action-packed, ironic segment of the pattern only after spending three acts detailing Easy's downfall.

A broader, more spacious work than any of the comedies

---

1. For critical opinion, see, for example, Eliot, p. 84; Ellis-Fermor, p. 131. For *A New Way,* see *Drama and Society,* pp. 273–80.

with which we have dealt, *A Trick* marks a further de-
parture from contemporary motifs and problems and from
a satirical stance. The pace here is brisker and the irony is
deeper and more complex, thanks to the intricate inter-
relationship of actions. A full discussion would be inde-
cipherable before a summary of the story, but one factor
needs noting here. Middleton splits the *senex* figure in two;
the young man, Witgood, finds himself opposed not only by
his uncle but also by his uncle's enemy, who has a niece
Witgood wants to marry. This complicates the action in
several ways. The young man has more obstacles to overcome, but his chance for ingenuity is greater. A whole new
area of action opens up between the two old men, who make
the most of the opportunity by being resourceful, wily, and
vastly entertaining. As a result, the play does not operate
so neatly as *Michaelmas Term*. It could be plotted as a
misshapen quadrilateral of forces working for and against
one another, with the young man's courtesan joining him
and the two old men as active scheming forces.

Despite differences in character configuration, the story
outline and cast of character types are similar to *Michaelmas
Term*'s. Like Richard Easy, Theodorus Witgood is a foolish young man, loser of lands and money. Easy was bilked
by his father-figure, Quomodo; Witgood's mortgaged lands
are held by his uncle, Pecunious Lucre. But similar situations can have different moral ramifications in action. Easy,
an innocent drawn into City life, does not do anything even
remotely dishonest. He is not an active trickster, dependent
as he is on Quomodo to fool himself.

Witgood has a different type of personality. He further
integrates the *eiron* figure into the action—is, in fact, the
chief mover of the play's intrigues. Destitute, unable to
marry the girl he loves, he enlists the aid of his whore and
his favorite bartender to trick his uncle into giving him
back his lands. The Host goes before him into the City,
proclaiming Witgood affianced to the "Widow Medler"—

the Courtesan, obviously—400 pounds a year strong in goods and lands.[2] Coached by Witgood, the "widow" instantly ignites the imaginations of the two old men.

Almost everything falls out according to plan. Lucre and Witgood's other creditors eagerly relieve his necessities, even advance him cash, as they look forward to having their outstanding obligations satisfied and devouring Witgood's new source of income. Hoard takes an even more direct approach, conniving to spite Lucre by marrying the widow himself. Witgood, using this opportunity to clear himself of his obligations to the girl, persuades her to accept the old man. Hoard discovers too late the kind of widow he has married.[3] Hoard is not alone in being tricked. All those who thought they would use Witgood are used by him instead. After the dust has settled, Lucre finds he has made his nephew his heir and returned his mortgages. Witgood's creditors have been paid off—at 13/4 to the pound, or even a little less—with Hoard maneuvered into footing the bill. Meanwhile, Witgood has married the girl he loves, Hoard's niece, without his consent.

Witgood's success is contrasted with the degeneration of the usurer, Harry Dampit, in three corrosive scenes placed between the actions of the main plot. When we first meet Dampit (I.iv), Witgood is at his nadir. But the relative positions change quickly. By the time the girl has eloped with Hoard and Witgood's plot has built a full head of steam, Dampit is on the brink of disaster (II.iv). He has a weakness for the bottle and is far gone in his cups. He shows a rather gay disregard for morality in his first appearance; here his railings at his servant Audrey are more somber. One wonders if the old one Dampit has tried and failed to trick is the devil himself, for the usurer goes to

---

2. The fruit of the medler looks like a small, brown apple. It is eaten when decayed to a soft, pulpy state. Cf. *As You Like It* III.ii.125 (OED).

3. There is much wordplay throughout the work on "Dutch widow," a contemporary term for whore. Marston's Franceschina was not a Dutch courtesan because of authorial whim.

bed swearing he smells burning horn. When Witgood has capped his triumph with his marriage, Dampit is at the point of death (IV.v). The atmosphere has become much more ominous; the watchers at his bedside want no part of him. Dampit reveals his own nature by calling his lieutenant "great Lucifer's little vicar" and departs, breathing his last to the crackle of hellfire, just before the conciliatory judgment scene.[4]

Most feel Dampit's scenes are chiefly satirical.[5] The usurer does seem to reflect a contemporary type, though attacks on lawyers and misers are literary commonplaces. At any rate Dampit is presented as a civil lawyer who had grown "rich by others laziness," having parlayed ten shillings into 10,000 pounds through hard work, unscrupulous dealings, and cozenages without number.

His sections of the play, only tenuously connected to the main plot, are rather disturbing. They are similar in tone to the satirical plays and quite out of keeping with the ruling spirit here. Middleton may have realized this, since he felt the need to get rid of Dampit before the final reconciliation. Some feel that he should have been kept out of the play altogether, but a case can be made for his presence.[6] For Richard Levin, Dampit serves as a sort of emotional lightning rod, drawing off from the more genial Lucre and Hoard the audience's antipathy to the usurer.[7] This view seems much more accurate than most. Some correlation can be made between Hoard, Lucre, and Dampit. But Levin

---

4. My account of the Dampit scenes owes much to Levin's ingenious analysis in *The Multiple Plot*, pp. 127–37.

5. But see *A Trick*, ed. Charles Barber (Edinburgh, 1968), p. 7. For this editor Dampit is "plainly intended as a figure of fun." He sees Dampit as a sort of roarer, who would fit more comfortably into *The Roaring Girl* than he does into this play.

6. *Ibid.;* Dampit "has no connection with the plot of the play." See also Barker, p. 57.

7. Levin, *The Multiple Plot*, pp. 126, 132. "Emotional lightning rod" is Levin's phrase.

also indicates that the Witgood action, in contrast to Dampit's story, is play existing in a moral and social vacuum, and
has a "pure" comic effect. This discounts Middleton's ironic
commentary as well as Witgood's forthright avowals of
reform. Although the Dampit plot is only one of several
commentaries on the morality of action in this play, it is
true that Middleton has restricted his overt moralizing to
this small part of the work, and that these patches of didacticism are worked into the play imperfectly.

At the least this marks an advance over *Michaelmas
Term,* in which a deal more than than three scenes are
marred by didacticism. In fact, the few snatches of satire
are lost amid *A Trick's* basic geniality. Middleton shows
more confidence here in the ability of characters and deeds
to speak for themselves. He guides the reader largely by
ironic juxtaposition of action and character within the traditional frame. The relation of the Dampit story to the
main plot shows a degree of symmetry. Witgood and the
Courtesan succeed, Dampit fails. The young people pit
their wits against those of two old men and win. Dampit
tries to outface an even older adversary, the devil himself,
and loses. Witgood seems more carefree next to Dampit,
Dampit more reprehensible next to Witgood.

Witgood, of course, the master spirit of the play, is far
more significant than Dampit and everyone else. Chastened
by experience, he shows a firm, authoritative intelligence,
and achieves a success remarkable in view of the number
and reputation of his opponents and the complexity of the
social situation. The central action, which he initiates and
guides, portrays his amazing regeneration, signified by his
entrance into adult society. He rises from the position of
dissipated "rake hell," the "spume of a brothel," to that of
successful trickster, landowner, husband, and sole heir to

his uncle. The Courtesan exhibits intelligence also, but her actions only counterpoint his: he puts her in a position to become respectable also.

Witgood's move to renew himself serves as catalyst for the regeneration of most of the City world. As a consequence of his labors significant change occurs in the life of each major character, except Dampit. As usual, the change is qualified. Though little is completely negative in Middleton's ironic plays, nothing is wholly positive. Good effects are weighed against bad, and gains ordinarily exceed losses. The young people improve their social position, gain stature and probity, though their virtue is damaged on the circuitous route they take to respectability. Lucre exults in Witgood's triumph over Hoard, but finds the operation has cost him his nephew's mortgages. Hoard wins from his enemies an intelligent but disreputable wife—at which Lucre registers dismay, then pleasure, Hoard pleasure, then dismay—and loses a virtuous niece, contributing to his opponents' victory.

The unsalvageable Dampit is eliminated and two deleterious relationships are righted. At the start Witgood and the Courtesan are man and whore, Lucre and Hoard are locked in ancient rivalry. The action shifts pairs, creating more wholesome combinations. The Courtesan and Hoard become bride and groom, Lucre and Witgood benefactor and heir. Witgood balances the marriage motif by marrying Hoard's niece, and the Courtesan becomes the logical heir of her ancient husband.

This involved symmetry reflects the complexity of the play world. Characters cannot be grouped in opposed City and country camps. *Michaelmas Term* depicted a bucolic countryside and corrupt City. The satires filled the streets and taverns with iniquity and made the chambers of the righteous refuges of grace and sanity. Except in the Dampit subplot, counters are not so univocal here. Witgood starts the play thoroughly debauched and destitute—in the country. Though he has all the marks of a City gallant, he obviously suffered part of his decline away from London, carousing with the Host, the "honest" country servingman. The Courtesan is also a country girl. The area outside London is no longer pictured as a place of innocent, idyllic retirement; in fact, Witgood leaves it to reclaim himself in the City, much as Easy had done the opposite, abandoned dull Essex to taste the excitement of the town.[8]

Relationships among characters are more complicated also. Witgood is a gentleman, Hoard a rich merchant, and Lucre expert in fiscal affairs; but classes do not always work one against another. Lucre is Witgood's uncle. Their family relationship reflects a truth of the Jacobean social situation, the intermarriage of gentry and merchants (unless, of course, Lucre is simply a gentleman in trade). Witgood becomes his uncle's heir whether he is gentleman or not; and the young man had turned to Lucre before, when he needed funds, though with disastrous results. Gallant Witgood also seeks to marry a merchant's niece, a girl with all the marks of a lady. Another marriage further accents social fluidity; Lucre raised his present wife, Jenny, out of an alderman's kitchen for "the raising of paste." Lucre has the last word on blood lines: "Most of our beginnings must be winked at" (IV.iii.79-80).

Witgood's struggle for Joyce, Hoard's niece, shows that wit is essential to successful functioning in such a complicated world. Joyce has other suitors besides Witgood: a rich fool and latter-day Sim Quomodo, Lucre's stepson Sam Freedom, and Moneylove, a poor philosopher. Hoard's brother Onesiphorus, oblivious of Witgood, asks which of the two would make a better match: "Pray, now, is not a rich fool better than a poor philosopher?" (I.ii.136-37).

8. *Mad World* and *Chaste Maid* further this complication of geography. Follywit leaves *Mad World*'s City to perpetrate his hoax at his grandfather's country estate. In *Chaste Maid,* the evil character who upsets the largely comfortable City world is a country knight, the aptly named Sir Walter Whorehound.

His companions think so, as do Hoard and Lucre, which confirms their mutual blindness. In Middleton wit is always more important than money. Poor "philosopher" always overcomes rich fool, gets the girl or the money, providing the poor man is a true philosopher, wise in deeds and not just in name.

Wit is better than riches because wit gets gold while gold cannot get wit. Middleton cares not so much about the amassing of wealth as he does about man's ability to cope with a world largely preoccupied with money and the forces that produce it. The young men have the same desires as the old men, but are intelligent enough to handle them more adequately. Although they are not interested in a career of poverty, they can put things in perspective. They move to fulfill their legitimate desires for land, wives, and security but limit their ambitions to a sufficiency, only enough to make them comfortable. They realize the limits of their deserts and abilities and know that cozenage on their part would breed it in others. The older men—Hoard, Lucre, Dampit, Quomodo, Whorehound—misjudge their capacity, snatch at everything, and lose it because they are not intelligent enough to match reach to grasp. Attitude toward possessions is more important than possessions themselves; greed and jealousy are to be avoided, if possible; not desire.

The prevalence of greed, jealousy, and avarice is a symptom of the sickness of Middleton's society and a warning of the need for wit sufficient to cope with it. When Witgood asks the Host if he wishes to help him, the Host responds:

Come forfeitures to a usurer, fees to an officer, punks to an host, and pigs to a parson desiredly? why, then, la.

(I.ii.17–19)

The encyclopedic effect here, the result of a desire to impugn the integrity of as many classes and types of people as possible, is a fixture of this and all the City Comedies.[9] However, Middleton does not revel in evil; it merely amazes and fascinates him. He admires man's ability to survive in a wicked world and celebrates those, like Witgood, who can do so without causing essential harm to others. The careers of his successful rogues exemplify the playwright's desire for a better society; for the young men and women always end the chain of evil. Though they strike back at their tormentors, they do not overdo it: the buck stops there.

The Courtesan, for instance, provides for herself without creating in Hoard a need for vengeance. His shame at marrying a whore does not run deep. The other characters provide the necessary consolation on the spot; and, as he will realize, he has actually picked up a tremendous asset, an intelligent and fetching girl who will be a testimony to his virility, an ornament to his house, and a nurse for his declining years.

Similarly, Witgood has the mercurial temper and evanescent moods of youth but is far from delinquency.[10] Though he guides his actions with a steady beam of enlightened self-interest, he is not overly egocentric. He shows sensitivity for others, even when the action grows hectic. When his Uncle grows disconsolate, he mollifies him by letting him in on the joke involved in Hoard's wedding. At times, he cannot bring himself to laugh at those he has tricked:

> *Lucre.* Gentlemen, I invite you all to my
> nephew's wedding against Thursday morning.
> *First Gentleman.* With all our hearts, and we shall
> joy to see

---

9. For further examples of his interest in the universality of evil in this play, see I.i.98–100; II.i.81–84 and 155–59; III.i.169–73 and 269–75; IV. iv.1–79; V.ii.51–55.

10. See I.i.1–97; the opening soliloquy and Witgood's consequent dialogue with the Courtesan exhibit marvelous modulations of tone and mood as well as fine, broad humor.

Your enemy so mock'd.
Lucre. He laugh'd at me, gentlemen; ha, ha, ha!
                         Exeunt all but WITGOOD
Witgood. He has no conscience, faith, would laugh
      at them:
They laugh at one another;
Who then can be so cruel? troth, not I;
I rather pity now, than ought envy?
I do conceive such joy in mine own happiness,
I have no leisure yet to laugh at their follies.
                                        (IV.ii.80–90)

In this play life is not wasted on the young, who know how
to make the most of it. The old men, who should be wise,
prove most foolish, their faults typical of old age. Cocksure
of his own ability, Lucre asks, "Am I a fool at fifty-four?"
(II.i.134), unaware that the question is not rhetorical. Such
conceit is lamentable, but fairly understandable. Both Lucre
and Hoard have been successful cozeners and have great
wealth to show as a sign of their abilities. Each has settled
into a rut, plotting the other's downfall from long practice,
seeing his opponent as the only obstacle to absolute su-
premacy in the field.

The habitual enmity of the City veterans is not only the
lever the astute Witgood uses to pry his way into society
but also one of *A Trick*'s central comic realities. We see
them as witty or apparently witty combatants rather than
as merchant-villains. Their chief epithet for each other is
"my adversary," the first words out of Lucre's mouth (II.
i.1). The protatic dialogue characterizes them not as canny
merchants but as ancient enemies:

      Onesiphorus Hoard.   His uncle and my brother
      Have been these three years mortal adversaries:
      Two old tough spirits, they seldom meet but fight,
      Or quarrel when 'tis calmest:
      I think their anger be the very fire
      That keeps their age alive.
                                        (I.i.112–18)

Each is jealous, but of the other's reputation, not his wealth. As Lucre admits, cozening is important to them less for its material rewards than for the proof of ascendancy it brings, and for the sheer joy of the game:

> The chief cause that invites me to do him most good is the sudden astonishing of old Hoard, my adversary: how pale his malice will look at my nephew's advancement! with what a dejected spirit he will behold his fortunes, whom but last day he proclaimed rioter, penurious makeshift, despised brothel-master! Ha, ha! 'twill do me more secret joy than my last purchase, more precious comfort than all these widow's revenues.
>
> (II.i.206–14)

The old rogues are punished little for their habitual (and delightful) iniquity. Middleton has been criticized for letting them off so lightly, but they hardly deserve severe punishment. Their foolish reveries of triumph are as preposterous and humorous as Quomodo's vision of the excursion to Essex. Nor are they completely irredeemable. They still exhibit considerable shrewdness, even if they are hampered by preconceptions; and neither acts exclusively for villainous reasons. Lucre is aware that Witgood is kin, even if his familial devotion is qualified. Witgood does become a pawn in the grudge match, but a special one because he is a relative. Nephew's success will redound to uncle's family pride as well as to his personal credit. Lucre sometimes assumes a tone that is, for him, philanthropic:

> Troth, he uses his uncle discourteously now: can he tell what I may do for him? goodness may come from me in a minute, that comes not in seven year again: he knows my humour; I am not so usually good; 'tis no small thing that draws kindness from me, he may know that (if) he will.
>
> (II.i.201–6)

The old man appreciates other values besides family ties. He genuinely likes the Host and praises, though mistakenly, his "honesty":

There's more true honesty in such a country servingman than in
a hundred of our cloak companions: I may well call 'em companions, for since blue coats have been turned into cloaks, we can
scarce know the man from the master.

(II.i.155–59)

Blue coats were the traditional costume of serving men.
That one can not tell master from servant is a double condemnation: of servants rising above their station, of masters
stooping beneath theirs. The remark is interesting as well
because it shows a sensitivity for right conduct and distinctions based on merit we might not have expected from
Lucre. The cozener himself is displeased to see a lowering
of social standards. However, the remark is flippant, to an
extent; class relationships are not of paramount importance
to Lucre. What does matter to him here is the Host's ability
to speak the truth, and more than that, to render an effective,
witty account of the widow and himself. Lucre shares Middleton's delight in people who can function in a world where
forthright action is difficult.

Lucre and Hoard hamper their own functioning by engaging in moral posturing. Each sees his riches as a sign of
virtue. In fact, Hoard twits Lucre on his nephew's dissolute
life, and Lucre admits that at least part of the boy's poor
reputation stems from his poverty. Economic security signifies moral excellence to the old men, and they are quick
to trumpet their own glory. A paradoxical situation indeed;
cozenage has allowed them to pretend probity.

Conversely, Witgood's poverty forces him to realize his
fallen condition. At the moment of awareness he initiates
a false action that maneuvers the old men into doing real
good, although they do not realize they are redeeming a
girl from whoredom and establishing a young man in his
rightful estate. Their success at trickery has bred smugness;
self-satisfaction allows more trickery to overcome it and
establish a more viable, productive society.

In this complex creation even those who lose, as Lucre does, can produce a credible logic for their actions:

> My adversary evermore twits me with my nephew, forsooth, my nephew: why may not a virtuous uncle have a dissolute nephew? What though he be a brotheller, a wastethrift, a common surfeiter, and to conclude, a beggar, must sin in him call up shame in me? Since we have no part in their follies, why should we have part in their infamies? For my strict hand toward his mortgage, that I deny not: I confess I had an uncle's pen'worth; let me seem half in half, true: I saw neither hope of his reclaiming, nor comfort in his being; and was it not then better bestowed upon his uncle than upon one of his aunts?—I need not say bawd, for every one knows what aunt stands for in the last translation.[11]
>
> (II.i.1–13)

His schemes are not terribly astute, but his perceptions are: his contention is not without merit. The boy was a surfeiter, brotheller, and "wastethrift." From his viewpoint, Lucre serves as avenging angel and custodian of the family property as well as canny operator. While goodness is often ironic in the play, evil always is. Hardly any action, then, is without its ambiguity.

Irony works throughout the play on several levels, quite significantly on the level of action. It is Witgood's task to pick his way through the City world's maze of conflicting desires and interests. On the simplest level we delight in contemplating Witgood's engaging the other characters in a game whose rules only he knows. But he is an excellent schemer as well as an architect; he foils unscheduled catastrophes as easily as those he can foresee. A dramatic presenter merged into the action, he can generally see his rival's moves, present and future, in his mind's eye. Instead of watching Gerardine or Fitzgrave watch the action, we see

---

11. "Aunt" was a slang term for whore (OED).

the action Witgood builds as he builds it, which makes for a much more organic drama.

The action reverses the thrust of the conventional matter of which it is made, something critics have seldom noticed. It is not in the natural order of things for City veterans to be swindled by such a neophyte as Witgood, especially since he uses ordinary coney-catching techniques. And at the *dé-nouement* the other characters are surprised to learn, though the careful reader is not, that Witgood's caper is essentially a positive act. He involved himself in villainy only so that he could retrieve his lands and put himself in a position to marry. He renounces evil and its pomps as a way of life at the beginning of the play and renews the pledge during it. As he insists during a scrape late in the action, his trick is a singular expedient:

> I perceive I must crave a little more aid from my wits: do but make shift for me this once, and I'll forswear ever to trouble you in the like fashion hereafter; I'll have better employment for you, and I live.
>
> (IV.iii.53–56)

Critical opinion has not often seen that here and in other Middleton comedies moral patterns sometimes correspond with economic patterns instead of being inverse to them. The young rogue's awareness of moral priorities increases with his success; as he acquires a stake in society, he realizes that social stability safeguards goods and lands, and accepts conventional attitudes and conduct more readily.

The roots of this acceptance lie in the rogue's attitude toward trickery. His dishonesty is sanctioned by the Old Testament notion of *quid pro quo:* one bad turn deserves another. Witgood has been tricked, almost robbed of his patrimony by an uncle who took advantage of his youthful inexperience. There is some justice in his turning tables and taking advantage of his adversary's age and expertise.

Moreover, to ignore the fact that Witgood does not see

cozenage as a permanent activity is to misunderstand the play. His are not the words or plans of one of a cast of characters who "are all of a piece—all scoundrels, all hopelessly and irretrievably bad."[12] Such a reading ignores precisely the most delicious aspect of the play's humor. Tricks are not just tricks here, but dishonest means of achieving justice. Witgood is attractive and fundamentally decent because he does not move about, as his elders do, trailing retainers and mouthing patently hypocritical pieties. His word is his bond, even if it is an unannounced promise to bring down the rotten pillars of the play community.

A few literary parallels highlight the redemptive nature of Witgood's actions. Surprisingly enough, Witgood bears some comparison with Prince Hal of Shakespeare's *1 Henry IV*. Both trick for the present and show themselves more worthy later. Though Witgood would not state it so grandly, he agrees with the Prince's plan of action:

> And like bright metal on a sullen ground,
> My reformation, glittering o'er my fault,
> Shall show more goodly, and attract more eyes,
> Than that which hath no foil to set it off.
> I'll so offend, to make offence a skill,
> Redeeming time when men think least I will.
> (*1 Henry IV*, I.ii.218–23)

Like all his actions, Witgood's redemption comes "when men think least [it] will." Hoard, Lucre, and the gentlemen who called him a "common rioter" at the beginning of the play are all astonished at his transformation at play's end.

Witgood and the Prince move in similar settings;[13] they have similar followers. Middleton seems fascinated with Falstaff, whom he copied in *Mad World* as well as here. Witgood's partner in trickery, the Host, with his love for "sack and ginger," good humor, and blunt honesty—the last ac-

---

12. Barker, p. 53.
13. Compare the tavern scenes, *1 Henry IV* II.iv and *A Trick* III.iii.

tually gross misrepresentation—shares qualities with the old knight. Like Falstaff, the Host is betrayed, left behind in the play world when the young man graduates to adult concerns. Like Hal, Witgood keeps his long-range intentions a secret from his companion, but not from the audience:

> *Host.* I knew't: shall we then see our merry days again?
> *Witgood.* Our merry nights—which ne'er shall be more seen.
> (*Aside.*
> (I.ii.63–66)

It seems significant that Middleton would echo and perhaps borrow from a play that has redemption and initiation into manhood as basic themes, even from a play as different from *A Trick* as *1 Henry IV.* The Prince shows himself as fine a calculator as his father, Witgood as skilled a trickster as his uncle, but only after each has been an excellent, highly comic wastrel. The parallel reveals to us an outlook and tone ordinarily denied Middleton's comedies as examples of "coterie" drama. There has been reluctance to see that characters of a Falstaffian stripe could appear in works not written by Dekker, Heywood, and Shakespeare.[14] But drama produced for the children's companies could be as full bodied, robust, and truly humorous as Dekker's and Shakespeare's plays.

This flavor is reflected in characterization. We have talked about how delightful the old men are, despite their abundant faults; the young people are even more winning. The Courtesan's name is a misnomer. Though many of the characters refer to her with disdain, we discover quite early that she is not without virtue. She always speaks the truth, betrays real affection for Witgood, and is quite intelligent. A forceful planner and organizer, she takes over Hoard's camp after their marriage. At every crisis, Hoard and entourage dither about until she tells them what must be done. She also has a sense of her own dignity and lets no

---

14. Harbage, p. 165.

one mistreat her. Lucre disputes Hoard's calling her a
common strumpet:

> Nay, now
> You wrong her, sir, if I were she, I'd have
> The law on you for that; I durst depose for her
> She ne'er had common use nor common thought.
> (V.ii.130–33)

Such admissions at the *dénouement* are sometimes meant to
be taken tongue in cheek, but nothing has happened to make
us doubt this one. The Courtesan has shown herself quite
an uncommon young woman.

She does not so much trick Hoard as allow him to trick
himself into making her honest. Her own actions are upright
enough, but she knows enough of the world, in its decadence,
to let it open a way for her. Throughout the plays we see
old men hewing to the letter of the law when the spirit of
their actions portends disaster for someone else. Here
tables are turned: Hoard fools people by saying what he
knows will be misunderstood, while the girl fools him by
saying just what she means. As she tells Hoard after their
marriage, she never did "boast of lands to you, money or
goods" (V.ii.140-41). Such honest speech is beyond the old
man's understanding.

Witgood has the same positive qualities as the girl; he
shows regard for her as she does for him. Though he
wishes to divest himself of her, he desires to see her honor-
ably and comfortably settled:

> Wench, make up thy fortunes now; do thyself a good turn once
> in thy days: he's rich in money, movables, and lands; marry him:
> he's an old doating fool, and that's worth all; marry him: 'twould
> be a great comfort to me to see thee do well, i' faith; marry
> him: 'twould ease my conscience well to see thee well bestowed;
> I have a care of thee, 'i faith.
> (III.i.115-21)

The young people are not blameless, of course. Their lowly condition at the start of the play is at least partly their own fault. They have allowed themselves to be used, have got themselves into a position from which only more trickery can free them. But at least they perceive the situation's irony. They are as aware of the moral ramifications of their actions as they are of the material benefits their scheme will produce.

The play celebrates the refusal of youth to be co-opted by age. It insists that society has room for individuals of different age groups and outlook. The problem of age's giving way to or making room for youth necessarily involves such questions as the relative value of experience and hard work, innocence and unconventionality; a good deal of the play's *brio* derives from its overthrowing conventional values.

The world is such that conventional wisdom is more often conventional than wise. What is closer to truth is often scoffed at as folly. Witgood and the Courtesan emerge from the play world reclaimed because they can separate habitual from wise conduct; appearance for them is not an absolute reality. For the old men it is. They have functioned too long within established patterns to sense when the time has come to readjust their behavior. The sagacity they have gained from a lifetime of experience is vitiated by faulty modes of perception. Self-satisfaction has rendered them vulnerable to assault, and the young people, catching them asleep, sweep past their positions to respectability. They cannot cope with Witgood because they are not able to realize that adversity has readied him for City combat; he has learned from his early errors.

The defeat of the old men is even more basic than this. They not only overestimate the folly of others but are also unable to gauge the extent of their own. When Hoard exults in his marriage, Lucre, unaware of the state of the bride's virtue, does not realize the joke is on Hoard:

> *Lucre.* O, master Hoard, your spite has watch'd the hour!
> You're excellent at vengeance, Master Hoard.
> *Hoard.* Ha, ha, ha!
> *Lucre.* I am the fool you laugh at:
> You are wise, sir, and know the seasons well.
> (IV.i.33–38)

Lucre's admission of folly is foolish, and Hoard is more foolish than he. Their damnation is compounded by Witgood's skill at getting them to indict themselves. Lucre, breaking from cover in his eagerness to capture the widow's fortune, says of Witgood:

> Why, do you think, i'faith, he was ever so simple to mortgage his lands to his uncle? or his uncle so unnatural to take the extremity of such a mortgage?
> (II.i.115–17)

Indeed, we do think so. Foolishness in Middleton has a marvelous capacity to tell tales on itself. The confessional tendency of fools in the later plays not only removes the sting of accusation but changes the object, and force, of the comic attack. We no longer scoff at the villain's evil, but laugh, with some sympathy, at his human fallibility.

The young are not easily wounded because they have awakened from their foolishness. They have accepted the world as it is—as Middleton urges us to do—and work within existential limits. They use available tools to achieve the possible. If trickery is the only avenue open to respectability, they embark on it but do not call it a high road. They know how to function in a world where ideal moral standards do not and cannot apply. In *A Trick*'s main plot Middleton implies values; he does not state them apodictically. That is the role of the older characters, who are minor or major scoundrels. Middleton shows us that a satisfactory life in a confused moral landscape is possible, but neither easy to achieve nor simple to appraise.

The better characters do cheat and fool others, but there are extenuating circumstances. Middleton's aspirant young people are always aware that theirs are perilous times, that men in general and their acquaintances in particular are not so honest as they could or should be:

> *Witgood.* I know the state of an old man's affection so well: if his nephew be poor indeed, why, he lets God alone with him; but if he be once rich, then he'll be the first man that helps him. *Courtesan.* 'Tis right the world; for, in these days, an old man's love to his kindred is like his kindness to his wife, 'tis always done before he comes at it.

(I.i.94–100)

However, the Host, Witgood, and the Courtesan aid one another because they have a mutual regard for their co-conspirators as fellow humans struggling for a place in society. They do not indulge in the name calling and hypocrisy Hoard cannot escape even in the last moments of the play.

It is the task of the young to revaluate the play world. They rephrase the play's misstated questions, adjust its mistaken assumptions. We have already discussed the Hoard family preference for rich fools over poor philosophers, a contention Witgood at once confirms and refutes by marrying Joyce and proving the Hoards rich fools and himself a rich philosopher. Once a poor fool himself, Witgood becomes through his "philosophy" of wit and code of conduct a prosperous landowner. Rich philosopher triumphs over fool again: new Witgood over old. Witgood also disproves one of his uncle's tenets. Lucre holds that a man who knows a woman a quean must be a knave. Knave himself, he does not recognize the "widow" as former quean. Witgood denies his major premise in action. In fact, he shows that knowledge of whoredom and knavery can be a handy tool in establishing respectability.

The play proposes and acts out a renewal of life, a transfer of power and purse from those concerned only with legal formalisms to those aware of law's spirit. The victors seek what law in and of itself, without humane interpretation, can never achieve, the enlarging and enrichment of life. Their attitude is far different from that of Lucre, who likes to "promise much and perform little" (II.i.269-70). They, instead, promise little, being of little promise themselves, but perform much. In them Middleton actualizes a comic vision replete with paradox: man is corrupt and sinful but can still do good; he must look out for his own welfare but can do it efficaciously while helping others; out of youthful folly can come the strength of maturity; out of mature success the follies of age.

Middleton's comic vision continuously looks in more than one direction. In a world turned upside down, even these affirmations can only be penultimate. For it is Lucre, of all people, speaking of his ne'er-do-well nephew, who affirms the truths most succinctly:

> *Lucre.* I grant he has been youthful; but is he not now reclaimed? mark you that, sir: has not your mistress, think you, been wanton in her youth? if men be wags, are there not women wag tails?
> *Host.* No doubt, sir.
> *Lucre.* Does not he return wisest that comes home whipt with his own follies?
> *Host.* Why, very true, sir.
>
> (II.i.81–88)

Of course, to turn the wheel one last time, he does not fully realize what he is saying.

5

A Mad World, My Masters

THE comic forms and themes of *Michaelmas Term* and *A Trick* continue to develop in *Mad World*. They are employed with the same skill here, but with a lighter touch. The most genial of the City Comedies, *Mad World* cannot easily be worked into a satiric or social warfare theory. For this or some other reason, critics have paid it scant attention.[1] This is regrettable, for the play is very enjoyable—in its main plot, at least, a subtle piece of work. The long, obvious judgment scene is eschewed in favor of the characters' rewarding and punishing themselves in ac-

---

1. There has been one article devoted to the play: William W. E. Slights, "The Trickster-Hero and Middleton's *A Mad World, My Masters*," *Comparative Drama* 3 (1969) : 87–98. I disagree with his contention, p. 93, that Middleton presents here "a world where thought and action, motive and consequence are totally unrelated." When they do mention the play, general studies give it only cursory treatment. See Barker, pp. 57–63; Gibbons, pp. 110–14; Holmes, pp. 46–48, 54. Levin, *The Multiple Plot*, deals with it mainly in connection with other plays, especially *Michaelmas Term;* see pp. 168–73 and 176–78. The only modern edition, ed. Standish Henning, Regents Renaissance Drama Series (Lincoln, Neb., 1965), is cited throughout the chapter.

tion. Familial roles grow even more complex here, and the victory of the young is qualified quite cleverly.

The plot resembles that of *A Trick* in basic detail. Richard Follywit, too, is a young man out of money; as the play opens he hatches a plan to get funds from his grandfather, Sir Bounteous Progress. He visits the hapless old man under a number of guises—visiting lord, courtesan, head of a dramatic troupe—and his schemes net him and his gang a considerable sum of money. But the trickster is stopped in full career, due to his own shortsightedness, when he is apprehended at grandfather's, booty in hand, after marrying the "chaste" Frank Gullman. His bride proves to have been Sir Bounteous's mistress, and the old man, completely triumphant, not only recovers his goods but can point to the courtesan as a memorial of his heir's foolishness.

This plot comes closer to pure fooling than anything else in Middleton, even though the action is quite meaningful and is handled with consummate irony. Curiously, this gayest of Middleton's stories is linked with a subplot among his harshest pieces of comic writing. The story details the efforts of Penitent Brothel, a "country gentleman," to suborn the wife of the citizen Harebrain. Gullman serves as go-between, linking the story tenuously but substantively to the main plot. Brothel has a good deal of success with Mistress Harebrain, largely because her husband is remarkably simple, until a succubus in her shape appears and frightens both of them into repentance.

Middleton has cast the two tales so that they have thematic and structural resonances, an achievement in itself. Although there is little surface similarity between this standard seduction scheme and the assortment of jest book gullings Follywit uses on his grandfather, the parallels are abundant. As Easy and Lethe were versions of the neophyte in a strange environment, so Brothel and Follywit are disadvantaged, one lacking women, the other money. Both move to make up their deficiencies, passively opposed by those with more legal right to the object than they. Both know their actions are wrong, though Follywit takes his "comic flashes" less seriously than Brothel, here, his "adulterous motions":

> But why in others do I check wild passions,
> And retain deadly follies in myself?
> I tax his youth of common receiv'd riot,
> Time's comic flashes, and the fruits of blood;
> And in myself soothe up adulterous motions,
> And such an appetite that I know damns me,
> Yet willingly embrace it. . . .
>
> (I.i.90–96)

Each employs accomplices in his scheme. Brothel is aided by a counterfeit virgin, Gullman, while Follywit has his boon companions—Mawworm, Ancient Hoboy, and the rest—as well as a counterfeit lord, himself disguised as "Lord Owemuch." Lust opposes chastity, thievery hospitality. Harebrain's jealousy and Progress's openhandedness are used similarly by their opponents. Since Harebrain's suspicion amounts to compulsion, Brothel can anticipate all his actions. Progress is an automatic entertainer, and Follywit works this admirable flaw for free lodging and access to his grandfather's goods. But both schemers see their plots crumble because of unforeseen circumstances, two less-than-saintly females. The succubus terrifies Brothel into chastity, while Gullman's "bashful maiden humours" enchant Follywit, who learns too late that they are the wiles of an accomplished prostitute.

The two stories do reinforce each other. An ironic balancing of elements increases the significance of each plot. Both actions reaffirm the viability of society. Brothel fails to destroy a marriage, Follywit embarks on a fairly good one: Grandfather forgives him and endows his bride, who is, after all, intelligent, resourceful, and attractive. We compare Brothel's serious though vicious attitude with

Follywit's playful, almost innocent one and draw our own conclusions.

Despite the parallels, it seems strange that Middleton coupled the stories. William Empson has shown that multiple plotting can set up an ironic counterplay of thought and emotion. The juxtaposition of contrasting plots allows us to indulge the "fundamental impulse of irony" to see the points of two opposed arguments, two sets of sympathies, to weigh the effectiveness of different types of conduct.[2] But the acceptance of dilemma that irony involves does not come easily here. The comparison by contrast does not act so efficaciously as that of *The Changeling* for instance. The main plot shows it is a mad world indeed, but the underplot ends on an unrelated, coldly rational note.

The characters and the stakes they play for differ fundamentally. Brothel's and Harebrain's game is quite serious; its prizes a wife and her affections, a husband's honor. Follywit's scheme is much more tolerable, because Sir Bounteous barely misses what the boy steals, money and goods already willed to him. Brothel and Mistress Harebrain must be changed radically before they can participate in the reconciliation that ends the play, and so their conversions precede final developments in the Follywit plot. Before his change of heart Brothel continually stops the action with self-conscious moral discourse, prejudging his evil actions in painful jog-trot couplets. The succubus is an even more unsatisfactory intrusion; Middleton wants us to consider adultery a hellish activity and puts a devil on stage to insure our getting the point.

Whatever the ultimate motive for its creation, this subplot sits uncomfortably beside the main action. It is a long jump from hell to the world of Dick Follywit, but Middleton asks us to make it.

---

2. William Empson, *English Pastoral Poetry* (New York, 1938), p. 62.

The bulk of the play depicts the schemes Follywit uses against his grandfather, foolery responsible for much of the play's carefree flavor. Follywit is harmless, as are his pranks. He and his gang set out not so much to rob Sir Bounteous as to draw an advance against the estate from an unwilling trustee:

> I know my grandsire has his will in a box, and has bequeath'd all to me when he can carry nothing away; but stood I in need of poor ten pounds now, by his will I should hang myself ere I should get it. There's no such word in his will, I warrant you, nor no such thought in his mind.
>
> (I.i.47–52)

The effort to fool Sir Bounteous is not a desperate venture. Follywit is much more secure and self-confident than Witgood. He and his lieutenants seem to move in a world of constant holiday; Follywit is certainly a Master of the Revels:

> *Hoboy.* What shall I call thee? The noble spark of bounty, the lifeblood of society!
> *Follywit.* Call me your forecast, you whoresons. When you come drunk out of a tavern, 'tis I must cast your plots into form still; 'tis I must manage the prank, or I'll not give a louse for the proceeding; I must let fly my civil fortunes, turn wild brain, lay my wits upo'th' tenters, you rascals, to maintain a company of villains whom I love in my very soul and conscience.
>
> (I.i.2–10)

In the play as in life, holiday exists within another order of being. Follywit is fooling with purpose. Like Prince Hal, whom he, too, faintly resembles,[3] the young rogue gradually emerges from holiday into a more sober, honest reality. However, redemption is not a constant theme. We can trace it in Follywit's first speech, quoted above, where he voices some dissatisfaction with his role as "forecast," a discontent

---

3. Compare the speech quoted above with one of Falstaff's, *1 Henry IV* III.iii.15–23. Mawworm and Ancient Hoboy bear a very faint resemblance to Bardolph, Ancient Pistol, and company.

submerged for most of the play. Quite late in the action it reappears, at first only implicitly, when Follywit thinks of marrying his "chaste virgin." But from the moment of matrimony, the redemption motif develops rapidly, an element of the play's general rush to completion. In the last lines we find Follywit protesting he is a new man, promising "hereafter stableness of life," and his actions there bear him out.

Follywit comports himself with insouciance, but his grandfather is the chief contributor to the play's geniality. Were Follywit's schemes aimed at anyone else, we could not take them so lightly. Sir Bounteous seems infinitely supplied with money and can forgive anything out of which he can extract humor. Although he has historical antecedents in the actual prodigality of country gentlemen, the old knight is a superb literary creation. Bounty and geniality flow from him as grease and good humor do from Ursula, the pig woman of Jonson's *Bartholomew Fair*. A humours character like Morose, he lives life according to one fixed idea, though his crochet of unbounded generosity makes this play much more sunny than *Epicoene*.

Sir Bounteous does not affect the action only through his predominant humour. He gives the play shape. Not competitor so much as play's center, he is the still point around which other characters revolve, striving to reach their goals. Follywit can impinge on the old man's consciousness only momentarily. Sir Bounteous lives life on a level infinitely wider, easier, more spacious than his grandson's. His very existence and Middleton's desire to create him form a commentary, perhaps the most valid one, on Follywit's fevered activity. If *Michaelmas Term* reveals the foolish roles in which youth is cast, *Mad World* presents the foolish roles youth picks for itself.

Considering Progress's wise acceptance and Follywit's

youthful foolishness leads us to the play's broader implications. The grandfather-grandson relationship and the transfer of the woman from older man to younger illustrates the play's social thrust. *Mad World* presents not a war to the death between classes, but the assertion of familial life and the conditions that make it possible. It depicts the constant struggle of the younger generation to establish itself at the expense of the older, or, better, to reach accommodation with it, which involves a process of growth on both sides. Progress is oblivious to Follywit's struggle; he holds the young man down not from choice but because he does not realize the boy's problems. Sir Bounteous should be aware of Follywit's need to live in the world. He also must be made to see both his grandson's new-found maturity and his own old age. His relationship with the Courtesan reveals the old man's refusal to recognize the inevitable. When she pretends illness he makes an egregious but characteristic error:

> Hark in thine ear, thou'rt breeding of young bones; I am afraid
> I have got thee with child, i'faith.
>
> (III.ii.38–39)

The putative mother's desertion ends his delusion and causes him momentary discomfort, shrugged off when he identifies the groom. The betrayal has had double effect. Sir Bounteous realizes his own indiscretion and begins to take note of his indiscreet heir:

> *Sir Bounteous.* Did she want anything? Was she not
> supplied?
> Nay, and liberally, for that's an old man's sin;
> We'll feast our lechery though we starve our kin.
>
> (IV.iii.88–90)

Accordingly, the thousand marks (about 600 pounds) with which he sweetens Gullman's marriage portion are owed as much to retribution as to compulsive generosity.

By the time of the marriage the old knight has received an education of sorts. He has seen his proper social role more clearly. His new knowledge leads him to answer and quiet with his gift Follywit's plaint that grandfathers hoard wealth others might use. This affirmation of social cohesion and vitality is highly ironic. In his tricks and disguises, Follywit abandons his own social position in order to engineer his grandfather into a proper role. The old man's liaison, a block to the aspiration of the young, was sterile in every sense. Sir Bounteous looks more satisfactory as *pater familias,* blessing the union of Gullman and Follywit, assenting to their entrance into the adult world.

Sir Bounteous's chief sin was that least blameworthy fault, omission. The young people did not have to work against him; rather they awakened his lively humanity to a more productive role and did even that inadvertently. The old man had been aware of his grandson's plight, though he did not try to alter the situation himself. He was willing to seek a position for the boy, even from "Lord Owemuch," Follywit in disguise:

> *Sir Bounteous.* I have a grandchild, my lord. I love him, and when I die I'll do somewhat for him. I'll tell your honor the worst of him: a wild lad he has been.
> *Follywit.* So we have been all, sir.
> *Sir Bounteous.* So we have been all indeed, my lord; I thank your lordship's assistance. Some comic pranks he has been guilty of, but I'll pawn my credit for him, an honest, trusty bosom.
> *Follywit.* And that's worth all, sir.
>
> (II.i.117–24)

The old man's good intentions cannot be denied, but his warm and generous acceptance of human folly was incomplete. Asking aid of comparative strangers was not enough. He had to be made to see that he should do something himself, while still alive, to help his kin.

This is just one example of the play's adjustment to the

standard Middleton notion of a world riddled with corruption. As Gullman's mother says:

> Every part of the world shoots up daily into more subtlety. The very spider weaves her cauls with more art and cunning to entrap the fly.
> The shallow ploughman can distinguish now
> 'Twixt simple truth and a dissembling brow,
> Your base mechanic fellow can spy out
> A weakness in a lord, and learns to flout.
>
> (I.i.140–46)[4]

The idea is viewed with nonchalance in the main plot; the subplot, however, takes it seriously, which must account for a good deal of its free-floating bitterness. Middleton was obviously unable to accept fully here an attitude of militant opposition to imperfection; the subplot does not work out a satisfactory dramatic response. The characters of the more successful main plot create a new comic world order while accepting the premise of the world's wickedness. They are quite imperfect themselves. Frank Gullman resembles the Courtesan of *A Trick* in intelligence, lively wit, and resourcefulness, but is much more experienced than she. If Gullman eventually lapses into virtue eagerly enough, she does come by the title "Courtesan" honestly.[5] Like his wife, Follywit is a convert to probity, saved by his falling in love. Before reclamation he goes his merry way, conniving for various reasons, none of them especially virtuous. Though he needs the money his schemes net him, the sternness necessity mothers is leavened by his attitude; for him trickery is fine sport as well as business. Though Follywit takes his pay, he is, in the truest sense, an amateur of his game. As Brothel says:

4. See also: I.ii.124–30; II.v.28–36; II.vi.59–64; III.i.39–46 and 103–15; III.ii.104–08; III.iii.48–62 and 88–97; IV.ii.18–25; IV.iii.92–101.

5. Frank Gullman looks much like Franceschina of Marston's *The Dutch Courtesan* as well. Compare I.i.149–59 with *The Dutch Courtesan*, ed. M. L. Wine, Regents Renaissance Drama Series (Lincoln, Neb., 1965), II.ii.10–18. See my "A Marston-Middleton Parallel," *N.&Q.*, forthcoming, December, 1973.

Here's a mad-brain o'th' first, whose pranks scorn to have precedents, to be second to any, or walk beneath any mad-cap's inven-
tions; h'as played more tricks than the cards can allow a man,
and of the last stamp, too; hating imitation, a fellow whose only
glory is to be prime of the company, to be sure of which he
maintains all the rest.

(I.i.82–88)

The attitudes of his characters do not imply that Middleton consents to evil or is careless about moral priorities. He
is a dramatist, not a lay preacher. In its main plot, *Mad
World* accepts the existence of evil but is not obsessed with
it. Wickedness here can be remedied. All the characters
eventually reject it, more or less convincingly, and turn to
new ways of life. Brothel undergoes a crashing conversion
when the nether world confronts him. Sir Bounteous for-
swears his foolish lechery after realizing that Gullman has
forsaken him, and why.

The change the young people undergo is more central
and convincing. The two rogues encounter each other and
discover the profits of virtue. Follywit is smitten by the girl's
beauty; love comes with first sight, and they have "clap't
up" within the hour. Maturation follows hard upon matrimony. Possessed of a wife and her dowry of 300 pounds,
Follywit is no longer so carefree about his roguery. A life
of crime has ramifications, as he discovers when he and his
sham players are checked in flight by a constable. From that
point on he uses his wit only to extricate himself from his
difficulties. He plans a different life. His wife echoes his
new sense of responsibility, protesting that she will be faithful in the future:

What I have been is past; be that forgiven,
And have a soul true both to thee and heaven.
(V.ii.259–60)

Characters who had lived only for themselves find an
advantage in working together. Their union is precipitous,

the girl's vow to reform a product of dramatic convention: still the match seems right. Marriage makes them both honest. By play's end they have worked together once, in fooling Sir Bounteous, and it is implied that they will continue to cooperate, for their mutual benefit. Each had expressed respect for honesty in the wild days, in almost identical terms.[6] Their marriage frees them to exercise this regard. Though the Harebrains' and Brothel's pledge of chaste friendship is less convincing, it does offer a variation on the theme.

Sir Bounteous, who stands alone in the play, is ready to extend understanding, forgiveness, and usually assistance to all. He is the play's strongest force for acceptance, for the realization that man must and will live, no matter how. Rules must be cast aside when they do not do justice to situation. When they do not and Progress falls afoul of some normally harsh reality—as when Follywit robs him to gain a livelihood—he licks his wounds and sees the humor in the situation. In the end he comes to realize the truth of Follywit's premise for putting the play world in motion:

> Let sires and grandsires keep us low, we must
> Live when they're flesh as well as when they're dust.
>   (II.ii.43–44)

Follywit's and Sir Bounteous's ethical attitudes are ultimately situational, as is the play's. Laws and rules present valid guidelines for conduct only when men find it possible to live under them. When they do not, they may and should go outside the limits of customary conduct, as Follywit does. In the main plot, at least, the play genially ridicules attitudes that would interpret law, stricture, and custom inflexibly. It asserts that custom must be put to the service of living, that rule must facilitate rather than impede life.

---

6. Follywit at II.i.124; Gullman at V.i.140. The statements are made under similar circumstances. Both gain emphasis from their position, one at the end of a scene, the other at the end of an important conversation.

The play does not oppose order. It reaffirms life but strives to place it in a chastened and no-less-reaffirmed social structure. Follywit gets his way for the most part: youth must be served, and is. But the young man's triumph is not clear-cut. His victory loses him the advantages of youth; he enters the world of adult conduct, whose limits have been strictly defined in the underplot.[7] Follywit asserts freedom but takes on new responsibilities. Society bends, letting him run wild, but is not broken. It is enlarged and renewed, and Follywit finds himself thoroughly caught up in the process.

This is only one of the play's ironies. That spirit is present throughout the play, informing even the title.[8] *"A Mad World, My Masters"* is at once a denial and assertion of order. "Mad" describes the world's fundamental disorder and illogicality; but the assertion of a "mad world," delivered to "my masters," implies an order of position, if not of worth, and the act of pronouncement itself insists that values still apply. The madness of Middleton's world is not to be rejected; it must be lived with because it is part of the very fabric of social life.

The title involves a relatively simple irony. The play deals with more complex patterns on levels of action and character. All the characters are ultimately indicted as fools. Most cannot understand others' actions or judge the implications of their own, and they continually play into the hands of those who would gull them.

Ironies in individual conduct are part of larger ironies informing the basic patterns of the play. As we have seen in Middletonian comedy, a controlling figure generally foresees and manipulates the conduct of others, jockeying them into paradoxical situations. Here Brothel, Gullman, and Follywit all have moments of control; and each of them is eventually tripped up by events, generally the very actions they have set in motion.

---

7. Henning, p. xi, feels the play depicts Follywit's last, unsuccessful stand against the adult world.
8. The implications of the title were first worked out, though to different effect, by Henning, p. x.

Follywit, the foremost manipulator, suffers the most significant reversal. As the play begins he approaches omnipotence; he proves Brothel's report that his pranks "scorn to have precedents, to be second to any" (I.i.83-84) by the ease with which, as "Owemuch," he robs Sir Bounteous and escapes. Though his schemes are continuously facile, the action gradually eludes his grasp. The first sign of slippage occurs after the Owemuch prank:

> Dost call't a muss? I am sure my grandsire ne'er got his money worse in his life than I got it from him. If ever he did cozen the simple, why I was born to revenge their quarrel; if ever oppress the widow, I, a fatherless child, have done as much for him. And so 'tis through the world either in jest or earnest. Let the usurer look for't; for craft recoils in the end, like an overcharg'd musket, and maims the very hand that puts fire to't.
>
> (III.iii.5–12)

Follywit had not delivered his opinions so assertively before. As might be expected, assurance leads directly to downfall. He learns that Sir Bounteous keeps a whore and considers her, for no apparent reason, a rival for his inheritance. First suspicious mood leads to first selfish act: while stealing the will made out in his favor he salves his fancied hurt by also taking a ring he later gives Gullman. Sight of the ring prompts the knight to drop the girl, helping Follywit do what he cannot achieve himself, separate Grandfather from drab. Once control is gone, the fabric of his scheme unravels. He marries his "rival," avoiding trouble in the best and worst way possible, by joining the opposition.

As position and prospects worry Follywit more, he is less able to manipulate events. They begin to double back on him, illustrating Middleton's delight in balance: the master fooler fails only when he indulges in the faults and stupidities of his dupes. Such a simple lesson, though, is too bald; defeat becomes victory as easily as victory defeat. Like Easy and Witgood, Follywit must experience foolishness before attaining wisdom. His actions end his career as

successful rogue but give him new life as functioning member of society, householder and heir to the Progress estate.
Follywit's fooler, Frank Gullman takes the same path. Never duped until she has tricked Follywit into marriage, she suddenly becomes myopic then. Not recognizing Follywit disguised as a player at Sir Bounteous's, she admits that she would love him were she unmarried, proving herself at once foolish and faithful. Her genuine refusal to consider a tryst with an actor reverses her pattern of conduct remarkably. She passes the test, although it is a false one. But in proving her faithfulness, she rejects the kind of man her husband has been. She avoids the liaison with a false image, the player, but embraces another shadow, Follywit as upright man. She searched for an honest man and unwittingly caught a rogue. Light dawns when Follywit is finally arrested. "Oh destiny!" she cries, "Have I married a thief, mother?" (V.ii.231). She has. Her attempt to make herself honest ends in union with one as dishonest as she.

Craft again catches craft, but the punishment is not excruciating. The rogue also happens to be heir to a fortune. The marriage of reformed rogue and reclaimed whore is blessed by Sir Bounteous. All our doubts about the feasibility of such an outcome are cast in shadow by the rosy glow suffusing the end of the play. There we see the happiest irony of all. Sir Bounteous, who has suffered at the hands of almost everyone—Gullman, Follywit, his lazy retainers—has the last laugh. The new Mistress Follywit's past will be a constant reminder of Grandfather's primacy and virility, however nonexistent that might be. His generous wedding gift reaffirms him as head of the family and asserts his sexual prowess:

> The best is, sirrah, you pledge none but me;
> And since I drink the top, take her; and hark,
> I spice the bottom with a thousand mark.
> (V.ii.262–64)

Ironies already discussed are redoubled by *The Slip*, the short, "sweet" dramatic production Follywit and company stage for Sir Bounteous and his guests late in the play. The world of *Mad World* is mad in relation to actuality; *The Slip* is mad in relation to the already mad world of the play. The playlet's plot is as counterfeit as its name is real.[9] Its scenario calls for nothing but Follywit's cheeky prologue covering the cast's quick getaway in rich attire borrowed from Sir Bounteous. However, the action prefigures Pirandello when a constable, unaware of the play-within-the-play, aptly but mistakenly checks the gang's escape. Follywit, an excellent ad libber, works the constable into the plot, binds him, and flees. Consistent in their overconfidence, he and his companions return later in their own shapes and are apprehended when a stolen prop, an alarm-watch, gives them away.

Follywit displays his formidable talents again but cannot outface fortune. Who can? The scene reveals the extent of everyone's foolishness. Sir Bounteous, of course, misgauges the actors' skill completely:

> Now up and now down, they know not when to play, where to play, nor what to play; not when to play for fearful fools, where to play for Puritan fools, nor what to play for critical fools.
>
> (V.i.29–33)

The players, on the contrary, have appraised their fools perfectly. At the end of the abbreviated performance, after the constable has been gagged and the thieves have run off, Sir Bounteous and Harebrain misjudge what they have seen:

> *Sir Bounteous.* Ha, ha, ha! By my troth, the maddest piece of justice, gentlemen, that ever was committed!
> *Harebrain.* I'll be sworn for the madness on't, sir.

---

9. Henning, p. 86n., feels that "slip" means counterfeit coin here. It might as easily mean the "escape" Follywit intends or the "error" he actually makes (OED). Middleton would surely be happy to have us see all three meanings.

Sir Bounteous. I am deceiv'd if this prove not a merry comedy and a witty.

(V.ii.113–16)

A merry comedy and a witty, indeed, but they should not be laughing. The audience does not know the actors are not fooling in their fooling. *The Slip* is counterfeit, but counterfeit by being serious. The thieving in the play-within-the-play is for real. Paradoxically, its humor lies exactly there: the thieves have the cheek to perform before their victims' eyes. Only gradually do the real fools, the audience on stage, come to their senses:

> *Sir Bounteous.* Gentlemen, shall I entreat a courtesy?
> *Harebrain.* What is't, sir?
> *Sir Bounteous.* Do not laugh at me seven year hence.
> *Penitent.* We should betray and laugh at our own folly then, for of my troth none here but was deceiv'd in't.
> *Sir Bounteous.* Faith, that's some comfort yet. Ha, ha, it was featly carried! Troth, I commend their wits! Before our faces make us asses, while we sit still and only laugh at ourselves.
> (V.ii.158–65)

But all is forgiven Follywit, including this last jest, because he is caught himself and possibly because he has taught the other characters such a valuable lesson. For this short episode reinforces the play's overriding assertion. In this mad world things are turned not only upside down, but inside out, until even the characters in a play do not recognize the truth of another play when they see it. Although actions do not always achieve what they merit, either for good or ill, the results are at times surprisingly apt, if gratuitous. Rogues who courted virgins marry whores, and whores trap rogues instead of honest men.

Despite the affirmation of Sir Bounteous's final forgiveness, there is more than a hint that the "mad world" will continue. After all, Follywit, "a fellow whose only glory is to be prime of the company" (I.i.87), is similar to his

grandfather in many ways. One can not help thinking that
Sir Bounteous's traits will live on in his grandson.

The play's final lesson, then, taught only by implication,
is that folly is universal. Its inevitability causes Follywit to
deride women and their habits while he dresses as one and
imitates them expertly (III.iii.90-115). It prompts him to
lie when he is trying to confirm his honesty:

> *Follywit.* Faith, grandsire, shall I be true to you?
> *Sir Bounteous.* I think 'tis time; thou'st been a thief already.
> *Follywit.* I, knowing the day of your feast and the natural in-
> clination you have to pleasure and pastime, presum'd upon your
> patience for a jest as well to prolong your days as—
> *Sir Bounteous.* Whoop! Why, then you took my chain along
> with you to prolong my days, did you?
>
> (V.ii.235–41)

But Sir Bounteous's whoop expresses joy as well as surprise. He is pleased by this jest, as he is by all the rest;
and he forgives Follywit, as the reader inevitably must.

No moral stigma attaches to this assent. The geniality
with which Follywit acts and the retribution that inevitably
catches him when he fails make it impossible to wish the
play had come out another way. After all, vice too is its
own reward, even in Follywit's case. Now husband and
householder as well as heir, Follywit has maneuvered himself into a position against which his own grandson will
probably rebel in turn.

6

A Chaste Maid in Cheapside

T HE last of Middleton's City Comedies is also the
most accomplished—the richest if not the most typical of his earlier plays. First performed between 1611 and
1613, by the same company that produced *Bartholomew
Fair,*[1] *Chaste Maid* stands a little apart from Middleton's
other works, as Jonson's play does from *Volpone* and *The
Alchemist.* Several years, at least five and possibly as many
as nine, had passed since Middleton had written his comedies for the children's companies. In the interim he collab-
orated with Dekker on the sentimental and topical play,
The Roaring Girl. Shortly before this work appeared Beaumont and Fletcher had begun to collaborate; their work
affected the taste of Jacobean audiences and dramatic style
to some degree. The influence of these events seems evident
in *Chaste Maid* in its sentimentality, its topicality, and in

---

1. Lady Elizabeth's Men. *Chaste Maid* was produced at the Swan; by
the time of *Bartholomew Fair*'s opening the company had moved to the
Hope. See E. K. Chambers, *The Elizabethan Stage* (Oxford, 1923), 2:
257–80; Barker, p. xxviii.

the sensational dueling scene between Touchwood Junior and Whorehound.

The play looks toward Middleton's future as well as back into his past. Here one can see signs of the Middleton who would later write pageants, tragicomedies, and two great tragedies.[2] Larger, looser, more character- and property-filled than the earlier works and yet more unified than they, *Chaste Maid* holds in solution more disparate elements than any other Jacobean comedy except, probably, *Bartholomew Fair*. Middleton's form is enriched here but is not changed; the themes and patterns seen throughout this study are varied and repeated in greater quantity and with greater skill and vivacity than before.

Chaste Maid stuffs its wide assortment of materials into four separate but meticulously paralleled stories.[3] Each involves the working out of triangular relationships between two men and a woman; the triangles fall into matched pairs, one concerned with youth and marriage, the other with older folk and adultery.[4] In the first relationship of the pair concerned with young people, Sir Walter Whorehound and Touchwood Junior vie for the hand of the chaste maid, Moll, daughter of the goldsmith Yellowhammer and his wife Maudline. Simultaneously Whorehound tries to pass off his Welsh whore as a "rich niece," worthy bride for Yellowhammer's simpleton student son, Tim. Both plots depict the opposition of older man, Whorehound, and younger—one young man intelligent, the other abysmally stupid. The whore is thought honest, the chaste maid a strumpet. The Yellowhammers come to regret Tim's match

---

2. Although I do not see as much as Samuel Schoenbaum does. See his "*A Chaste Maid in Cheapside* and Middleton's City Comedy," *Studies in the English Renaissance Drama*, ed. J. W. Bennett *et al.*, (New York, 1959), pp. 287–309.

3. The matter tends to be "stock material" in use for "at least a century." See *Chaste Maid*, The Revels Plays, ed. R. B. Parker (London. 1969), p. xxxv. Citations of the text are from this edition.

4. I am indebted here to Richard Levin, *The Multiple Plot*, pp. 194–202. Much of the hard information is taken from that study, though our constructions of events differ.

with the Welsh woman, which they promoted, and to
approve Moll's union with Touchwood Junior, which they
tried to block. For dowry the fool gets the whore's nineteen
"mountains" and 2,000 nonexistent "runts," the clever gallant the chaste maid's 2,000 pounds.

The remaining triangles, involving more mature matri-
monial relationships, are equally well balanced. One concerns Sir Walter and the Allwits, with whom the Knight
dwells when he is in town, cuckolding Allwit, even siring
his children, to everyone's satisfaction. Allwit lives as a
guest at home, ceding Sir Walter such painful tasks as
raising the children and keeping a jealous watch over his
wife. The last triangle treats the affair of Sir Oliver and
Lady Kix and another interloper, Touchwood Junior's
brother. The barren Kixes need a son in order to inherit
property that would otherwise fall to their relative, Sir
Walter. With Touchwood Junior's support, Touchwood
Senior contracts to provide the Kixes with an infallible
fertility potion. Copying the scheme of Machiavelli's *Mandragola,* he impregnates Lady Kix himself. The "potion"
works, and Lady Kix's condition has triple effect: the Kixes
get the land; Sir Walter, his hopes ruined, is arrested for
debt and abandoned by the Allwits; Sir Oliver, convinced
of his potency, rewards Touchwood Senior by establishing
him and his family in the Kixes' house. An action destroying
one unholy triangle sets up another. Allwit discards the role
of cuckold to become head of his own household, full of
children and movables. Sir Oliver's house will probably fill
with children also; but he is unaware of his status, while
Allwit was scandalously conscious of his. Sir Walter, who
curses his offspring, is cast out; Touchwood Senior, who
produces children for Kix so that he can provide for his
own, is taken in. Sir Walter, begetter and rejecter of
bastards, is disinherited by Touchwood's producing a bas-
tard, accepted by Sir Oliver as legitimate.

Sir Walter, the primary character connective between

plots, is actively involved in three of them and affected by the outcome of the fourth. His arrival from the country puts the play in motion and his expulsion occasions its close. Other factors contribute to the work's coherence as well. The play abounds with familial and familiar relationships. Tim and Moll, of course, are brother and sister. The Touchwood brothers participate in each other's adventures, younger preparing older for his treatment of Lady Kix, Senior helping Junior in his attempts to steal Moll. Sir Walter knows Touchwood Senior (both have been in town seven years) and Touchwood Junior and Moll serve as godparents for the Allwits' and Whorehound's latest child. In turn, the Allwits, along with their acquaintances, the Kixes, attend the lovers' "funeral"-marriage. Lady Kix is present at the christening of the Allwits' infant, despite her forlorn comparison of Mistress Allwit's seven children with her own seven years of barrenness.

The elaborate network of correspondences does not make the play seem schematic. Part of the reason is the gay abandon with which Middleton skips from plot to plot, but something is owed to the play's ability to hold heterogeneous elements in solution. Several set pieces—the christening scene, the trick played on the Lenten promoters, the jest book inspired episode of the porter—are worked into the fabric of the play. Though they have little necessary connection with the plots, these vignettes do not slow down the action so much as counterpoint it. The main stories vary widely in tone.[5] The Moll-Touchwood Junior plot is romantic, sentimental, at times almost mawkish; its gratuitous danger and arbitrary reversal would look at home in *The Maid's Tragedy* or *A King and No King*. This seriocomic tale balances the low broad humor of the story of Tim and

---

5. Though not so systematically as Levin suggests. He classifies Moll and Touchwood Junior's story as serious-sympathetic; Allwit's serious-unsympathetic; Kix's farcical but sympathetic; and Tim's farcical and unsympathetic. See *The Multiple Plot,* p. 200.

his bride, in which Middleton indulges his taste for pseudo-learning and spurious logical disputation. The story fairly runs amok with debased Latin, low-grade logic, and broad digs at the Welsh. The gusto of Tim and his tutor save the plot from narrow, arid pedantry. Here Middleton has finally perfected a type he experimented with earlier: Tim far surpasses Sim Quomodo and Sam Freedom in excellence as a learned lunkhead, if not in real knowledge.

The cuckolding plots each have a distinct flavor as well. The Allwit story is at times efficient and calculated, though it shows a great deal of good humor. We laugh at Allwit's sheer audacity as well as at his wit; however, the comedy he creates is clever rather than joyous. By contrast the Kixes are singularly carefree and innocent. Even their frequent arguments are marvels of good fun. Though the plot has literary origins, it involves earthy, human situations, such as the Kixes' vigorously accusing each other of sterility. Despite their bickering, they are genuinely fond of each other; and Sir Oliver's sheer pleasure at the appearance of an heir makes it difficult to feel the potion has had other than salutary effect.

Despite the play's evident coherence, there has been some discussion in recent years about what gives it unity. Two recent studies reverse priorities by approaching the play as a poem.[6] They show convincingly that such recurrent images as flesh, blood, and the overtly sexual puns and symbols help unify the action. But treating drama as poetry ignores the vital fact that a play can be a working out in action of conflict between characters espousing different styles or philosophies. Characters enunciate theme and pattern, which are prior to and encompass imagery and figures of rhetoric.

---

6. Ruby Chatterji, "Theme, Imagery, and Unity in *A Chaste Maid in Cheapside,*" *Renaissance Drama,* ed. Samuel Schoenbaum (Evanston, 1965), 8:105–26; *Chaste Maid,* ed. Parker, pp. xlv–lxvi. Both studies seem reactions to Levin's structural approach. See notes 4 and 5.

The action is organized around the working out of several paradoxes. In each case actuality as embodied in particular characters modifies or overthrows preconceptions sanctioned by common usage, legality, or custom. New life drives against the barrier of life-style encrusted with age, solidified by habit and success.

The basic character configuration of the play is the family, and within each family unit we find members opting for different sides of the various paradoxes. The play resolves and rearranges family units while working out its situations. Almost all the families are caught up in each dilemma to some degree, complicating and enriching the play further.

The comedy's first paradox is expressed in its title, which a London audience of the day would find a joke in itself. As R. B. Parker tells us, the women ordinarily "chased" in Cheapside were prostitutes, who might be whipped through it at cart's tail.[7] Like Cheapside, the play is full of disreputable women. Touchwood Senior's wife is the only chaste woman in the play besides Moll. Allwit's wife, Lady Kix, and the Welsh "gentlewoman" are all of easy virtue. Even Maudline Yellowhammer seems to have grown respectable only since her marriage:

> *Maudline.* I hold my life you have forgot your
> dancing:
> When was the dancer with you?
> *Moll.*   The last week.
> *Maudline.*   Last week!
> When I was of your bord, he miss'd me not a night;
> I was kept at it; I took delight to learn,
> And he to teach me; pretty brown gentleman,
> He took pleasure in my company. . . .
>   (I.i.14–19)

She is hardly scrupulous about her daughter's virtue either. In effect, she and Yellowhammer try to sell Moll. The dilemma of the title story is whether Moll will be married

---

7. Parker ed., p. xlvii.

off profitably, or romantically and chastely. The Yellowhammers would prostitute her and her 2,000 pound dowry
for the social position and imagined respectability an alliance with Sir Walter would bring.

Almost nothing can make Yellowhammer wary of the
deal. When Allwit tries to break up the match for reasons
of his own, his news that Whorehound is an "arrant whore-
master" moves Yellowhammer, but only to preserve the
integrity of his ware:

> The knight is rich, he shall be my son-in-law;
> No matter, so the whore he keeps be wholesome,
> My daughter takes no hurt then; so let them wed:
> I'll make him sweat well ere they go to bed.
>   (IV.i.247–50)

The merchant grants the knight's deeds may be "black,"
but decides that marriage "calls them back," or covers
them with a cloak of probity. This attitude toward Moll
is a mark of her parents' inversion of values. When her
second effort to escape fails, Moll is dragged across the
stage by her hair, a singular mark of disgrace. Yellowhammer calls her "impudent strumpet" and Tim makes
lewd remarks about her (IV.iv.25-28). She merits the epithet "strumpet" because she refuses to be merchandised. A
confirmed mercantilist, the Welsh woman is constantly called
"gentlewoman," a title Yellowhammer tells Touchwood
Junior is inappropriate for his daughter (I.i.180-81).

Despite her parents' opposition, Moll finally marries as
she wishes. Even the Yellowhammers finally recognize the
value of a love match (V.iv.57-59) when they discover that
Tim's wife is no bargain, in any sense. The shock of the
title's joke, a chaste maid in—*Cheapside!,* is redoubled by
this successful vindication of the girl's chastity. After all,
even more audacious than the "very idea" is the embodi-
ment of chastity in Cheapside, especially when the paradox
is tenaciously worked out amid several unchaste actions.

Middleton accents the joke's importance by emphasizing its resolution. Most of the impure characters attend and approve of Moll's wedding. They bear witness to rejection of the very activities in which they indulge. The bridegroom's emergence into a new life and the young couple's assertion of love as an operative force come as a burst of joy after the gloom of the highly conventional trick that finally frees them to marry, their mock death and funeral.

The transition from sadness to joy is vivid because Middleton carefully plans the funeral scene; its stage directions, the most elaborate in the play, emphasize the solemnity of the occasion. Though Touchwood Senior's eulogy betrays a trace of burlesque—which only increases the audience's expectation of a happy recovery—his remarks are serious at core:

> Never could death boast of a richer prize
> From the first parent; let the world bring forth
> A pair of truer hearts. To speak but truth
> Of this departed gentleman, in a brother
> Might, by hard censure, be call'd flattery,
> Which makes me rather silent in his right
> Than so to be deliver'd to the thoughts
> Of any envious hearer, starved in virtue,
> And therefore pining to hear others thrive. . . .
> (V.iv.1–9)

Such a speech, delivered in the play's final scene, increases the affirmation of marriage embodied in the young people's union. But the situation is not without irony. The paradox of chastity in Cheapside or, rather, in an unchaste world, is both resolved and reinforced. I do not speak of the unchaste characters' assent to the match, which would be expected for both social and dramatic reasons, nor of the argument that the assent and the ceremony's solemnity are *pro forma,* that the young people will probably be drawn into the corrupt world around them before long. We need not go beyond the wedding scene itself and its chief architect to find factors that increase rather than lessen the situation's complexity.

Touchwood Senior, who plans and participates in the wedding scene, is also the play's most lecherous figure. As much fertility symbol as character, he is forced to break up his own household because he produces more children than he can support.[8] When he exercises himself outside marriage, which he must often do, he is so overwhelmingly potent that he inhibits nature itself, impeding the harvest because so many farm girls must harvest crops of his sowing (II.i.60-62). Even his name is a bawdy pun on his unusual powers.[9]

In addition to arranging the ceremony itself, Touchwood Senior helps clear the path for the marriage. He cuckolds Sir Oliver partially at his brother's request, committing adultery to make a chaste union possible. Threatened chastity is preserved and a chaste couple established by the very act that sets up what could be a permanently adulterous menage: Sir Oliver invites Touchwood Senior's family into his home only a moment after he has bestowed his blessing on the newlyweds.

Sir Oliver's too kind offer to Touchwood has other ramifications as well. Cuckolding Sir Oliver also makes it possible for Touchwood Senior to set up housekeeping again with his own chaste wife, reestablishing another healthy union. The Touchwoods had separated partially for financial reasons, but the welfare of their children concerned them much more than the commercial considerations that engaged the Yellowhammers. The Touchwoods would rather endure the "tediousness" of separation than produce a child "sure of beggary" (II.i.1-3, 35).

---

8. For an extended discussion of the notion of fertility in the play, see Arthur F. Marotti, "Fertility and Comic Form in *A Chaste Maid in Cheapside*," *Comparative Drama* 3(1969):65–74.

9. "Touchwood" means tinder, especially that used to ignite the touch hole of a musket. Richard Levin, "Middleton's Way with Names in *A Chaste Maid in Cheapside*," *N. & Q.*, n.s. 12 (1965):102–3.

Touchwood Senior does not represent only sexual abandon. His views on his wife's restraint bespeak part of his attitude:

> This does not only make her honesty perfect,
> But her discretion, and approves her judgment.
> Had her desires been wanton, they'd been blameless
> In being lawful ever, but of all creatures
> I hold that wife a most unmatched treasure
> That can unto her fortunes fix her pleasure
> And not unto her blood. . . .
>
> (II.i.43–49)

In this context his actions become even more ironic. Like Witgood he may be involving himself in shady dealings only so that he can free himself from them. Here and elsewhere we sense his real appreciation of marriage and fidelity. Moreover, he cuckolds Sir Oliver not so much for pleasure as for a number of business and charitable reasons. His wish to assist his brother is a motive, but the 400-pound reward offered by Sir Oliver is a prior consideration. Presumably this sizable sum would have helped him reestablish his household had Sir Oliver not issued his invitation.

Sir Oliver's generosity resolves a minor dilemma related to chastity and sexual activity. Touchwood Senior had lamented:

> Some only can get riches and no children,
> We only can get children and no riches!
> (II.i.11–12)

In his new circumstances Touchwood Senior's "gift" will not have harmful effect even if he should not reform. The new Touchwood-Kix household will have the best of both worlds: Kix will supply all the riches, Touchwood all the potency either family needs.

The other pair of plots follow the same pattern of dissolution and resolution, negation and affirmation in dealing with the chastity-promiscuity polarity. The Allwits are freed from the deleterious influence of Whorehound, who lies in debtors' prison as the other characters celebrate the play's marriages. This does not, however, necessarily confirm the triumph of chastity; there are strong hints that the Allwits are about to set up a bawdy house on their own.[10] But that is left to the future. In the final scene Allwit is one of the principal speakers of choric asides and comments approving the chaste maid's chaste match. He and his wife take their place, for the moment, in the ranks of more or less respectable married couples watching Tim rationalize his marital dilemma. The young pedant caught himself in another paradox, claiming he could prove a whore an honest woman. He does so all too inadvertently by marrying Whorehound's Courtesan. He wins his point, but his mother is more correct in asserting that a whore must prove herself an honest woman. The whore agrees, making the classic promise of Middleton's newly wed queans: "There's a thing call'd marriage, and that makes me honest" (V.iv.106).

The play does not completely resolve the larger paradox but does state it cleverly and comically. Chastity and adultery intertwine in action, but the work is essentially affirmative in trying to clarify its sexual relationships. If the stasis at play's end is temporary, it is still a point of resolve in each plot. Honest women are proved whores, but the play witnesses Moll's and Tim's marriages, the settling of real and imagined inheritances, and the clarification of two unions that had been laboring under economic or moral difficulty. A chaste love culminates in marriage, and a barren match is made fruitful. Mistress Allwit and the Welsh woman have been extricated from whoredom, perhaps only conditionally, and Moll has been saved from a mercenary

---

10. Parker ed., p. 104n. Parker notes that "the Strand seems also to have been notorious for courtezans . . . ," citing literary references. Allwit's citing of the "quaint and costly" materials with which they will deck the house seems indicative of the house's nature.

alliance. If Lady Kix has been compromised, she has at least been given a child, and her relationship with her husband seems far more serene. In all the relationships generation will be rendered more efficacious. Three women have been saved from Whorehound, who has no regard for his children. Moll and the whore have been matched with mates closer to their own ages and circumstances. And though Tim's marriage is less prepossessing than Moll's, he seems determined to make the best of it. Of course, Touchwood Senior has been put in a position where he can work with a will, apparently without doing anyone especial harm.

Chastity may or may not be preserved; one must reckon with the results when it is not. Here lies the next paradox. Awash with flesh, the play takes place during Lent and is set, in part, in a meat market.[11] *Chaste Maid* devotes itself to the problem of desire and of dealing with desire's occasional result. More often than not "flesh" refers here to the human body and flesh is always related to "blood," sexual desire. Flesh means "food," primarily, only in the Lenten promoters' scene, where the reference is not unambiguous. Many of the characters must come to grips with the problem presented by flesh and blood. Touchwood Junior's solution is a truly Lenten one:

> *Moll.*   Sir?
> *Touchwood Junior.*   Turn not to me
> Till thou mayst lawfully; it but whets
> My stomach, which is too sharp-set already.
>   (I.i.139–41)

But there are several other possible remedies.
Touchwood Senior follows his brother's line in part, ab-

---

11. *Ibid.,* p. xlvii. Allwit's house, overlooking Pissing Conduit, must be located in the "Stocks" meat market. Thus it would be at one end of the City's chief radial artery, with Yellowhammer's shop at the other end.

staining from sex in marriage; however, he breaks his fast with Lady Kix. This violates Lenten regulations and traditional moral standards, but Middleton does not withhold absolution: the Lady Kix-Touchwood Senior relationship is the only illegitimate liaison not upset by play's end, a mark of some favor. The ethical considerations in force here are predicated on Touchwood Senior's attitude toward his own marriage:

> The feast of marriage is not lust but love
> And care of the estate; when I please blood,
> Merely I sing and suck out others'. . . .
>
> (II.i.50–52)

Socially centered love is concerned with wife and family, object of love as well as subject. Touchwood Senior's administering his "potion" does not merely "please blood"; it cares for his and for Sir Oliver's estate. Though he invades Sir Oliver's prerogatives, perhaps permanently, the old man and his family are the better for it. Sir Oliver, obviously and comically past the age of fleshly accomplishment, has no "blood" to "suck out." The Kixes' barrenness is the only source of friction between them; when Lady Kix asks Touchwood to bring them into love again, he does, even if his methods are unorthodox. Sir Oliver's wish will come true:

> I hope to see thee, wench, within these few years,
> Circled with children, pranking up a girl,
> And putting jewels in their little ears;
> Fine sport, i' faith!
>
> (III.iii.90–93)

If this scene is made possible only at the cost of Sir Oliver's wearing horns, the trick hurts no one. Sir Oliver himself is not aware of the situation, and there is no reason for Lady Kix or Touchwood to enlighten him. The problem's solution is comic and immoral, but attractive enough.

While others are faced with the problem of excess flesh, the Kixes are only too pleased to get flesh after years of "drouth and coldness." It is basically healthy for Lady Kix to break her seven years' fast, even if she does it during Lent.

Before Touchwood Senior can move into his new household, he must put his affairs in order. Much flesh already produced must be disposed of. He deals with the problem in the Country Wench's episodes, scenes partially responsible for the critical notion that the play's tone is harsh and essentially misanthropic.[12] The bare outline of her story seems chilling enough. The country girl approaches Touchwood with a child he fathered. He gives her money and tells her to place the child somewhere. She does, by hiding the child in a basket of meat confiscated by the Lenten promoters, the city's monitors of the meat trade. The deed sounds inhuman but is incontestably funny in context. Considered as one action related to others, the jest makes a positive statement on social values, a contribution to the play thematically.

As in the case of the Kixes, situational exigency dictates the nature of proper conduct. Touchwood Senior and the Wench act as they do because they can do no better under the circumstances. Touchwood helps the girl as much as he can, giving her his ready cash and suggesting ways of placing the child. The girl believes he is doing his utmost, and the reader does too, because the encounter immediately follows the breakup of his household. Times are hard for the girl and Touchwood, not a little because they are dealing with hard people. The situation is ultimately humorous not because a baby is abandoned but because the promoters —who are supposed to enforce Lenten regulations but

---

12. See, for example, Schoenbaum, "*Chaste Maid,*" p. 289. A more persuasive view is proposed by Robert I. Williams, "Machiavelli's *Mandragola,* Touchwood Senior, and the Comedy of Middleton's *A Chaste Maid in Cheapside,*" *SEL* 10(1970) : 388–89.

actually divert confiscated meat to their own use—richly deserve the trick played on them.

Middleton sets the scene for the Wench's entrance meticulously, exposing the Promoters' corruption in a series of *lazzi*. Allwit slips off after fooling them into thinking he is smuggling meat. Another man enters, tries to sneak by them, and fails. Then another. After that the Wench enters. By this time the situation cries out for reversal, aesthetically and morally, and the Wench provides relief with a vengeance. She makes no attempt to trick the Promoters, who by this time are swaggering with success, but flaunts her basket and falls into their hands. Before she gives up the basket, she makes the Promoters promise to keep it until she returns. They are only too glad to agree and rue it as soon as they examine what they thought was a lamb's head. In finding the baby they are cheated of the meat they expected and saddled with a piece of flesh they can neither use nor dispose of:

> 2 *Promoter.* Here's an unlucky breakfast!
> 1 *Promoter.*   What shall's do?
> 2 *Promoter.* The quean made us swear to keep it
>   too.
> 1 *Promoter.* We might leave it else.
> 2 *Promoter.*   Villainous strange!
> Life, had she none to gall but poor promoters
> That watch hard for a living?
> 1 *Promoter.*   Half our gettings
> Must run in sugar-sops and nurses' wages now,
> Besides many a pound of soap and tallow;
> We have need to get loins of mutton still,
> To save suet to change for candles.
>   (II.ii.157–65)

The significances of trick and response are multiple. Part of the humor springs directly from the Promoters' confused notion of honor. They are quite willing to use their post for personal profit but feel they cannot break their word. What one says in comedy can have exaggerated importance, and the promise to keep the basket and its contents binds them completely. Wont to steal flesh from the unwilling, they are tricked into a bundle of flesh by a cheerful giver. Before their mishap, the Promoters calculated how they would dispose of the food they had confiscated. After, they must plan how to nourish the live flesh foisted off on them and leave stage planning to put their charge out to nurse. In chastising the Promoters, the Wench has found a home for her child and awakened in them some sense of humanity. Like Touchwood in getting children but no riches, she shifts the buden of parenthood to those who get riches but no children and ordinarily inhibit rather than promote life.

Attitudes toward children, one's flesh and blood, are important throughout the play, almost a touchstone by which to judge the various characters. We enjoy the Wench's agility in providing for her child and admire Touchwood Senior's economy in establishing both his family and Sir Oliver's. The Yellowhammers do not evoke the same response. We have already discussed their attitude toward Moll; significantly, they think they are getting as well as giving flesh:

> *Maudline.* You had need have somewhat to quicken
> Your green sickness—do you weep?—a husband!
> Had not such a piece of flesh been ordained,
> What had us wives been good for?
>
> (I.i.4–7)

Allwit and Whorehound also offer a contrast in attitudes toward children. There has been a tendency to see Allwit in a dark light,[13] but he can certainly be regarded favorably here. He is quite fond of his wife's children even if he did not sire them; the new-born girl gives him special pride:

---

13. See Levin, *The Multiple Plot,* p. 197; Chatterji, p. 113.

Allwit. Let's see her once again; I cannot choose
But buss her thrice an hour.
Wet Nurse.   You may be proud on't, sir;
'Tis the best piece of work that e'er you did.
Allwit. Think'st thou so, nurse? What sayest to Wat
     and Nick?
Wet Nurse. They're pretty children both, but here's
     a wench
Will be a knocker.
Allwit. (*Dandling child.*)   Pup!—Say'st thou me
     so?—Pup, little countess!
Faith, sir, I thank your worship for this girl
Ten thousand times and upward.
Sir Walter.   I am glad
I have her for you, sir.

                                    (II.ii.18–28)

When Sir Walter lies wounded, Allwit tells the boys, Wat
and Nick, to comfort him and is shocked to see them rejected. One reason for the Allwits' final disavowal of
Whorehound could be his rebuffing the children. The Allwits are somewhat venal, but Sir Walter is much more
selfish than they. Afraid he is about to die, wrapped in his
own fate, his only legacy to his offspring is curses. Sir
Walter's attitude surprises the Allwits but not the reader.
Quite early the knight had decided to put the boys out to
trade, should he marry, instead of introducing them into his
family (I.ii.109-17).

Though Tim Yellowhammer comes up from Cambridge
about halfway through the play, he still makes a sizable
contribution to it. He proposes the comedy's central paradox, that *"Stultus est animal ratione,"* a fool is a rational
animal. Tim is the play's paramount fool. His very reasoning of this and other paradoxes is foolish, for his philosoph-
ical equipment is limited to *negantur argumenta* and defec-
tive syllogisms. In a rare burst of good sense, his mother

shows that he and his Tutor are trapped in their logic and cannot discern truth. She argues that a fool is "one that's married before he has wit" (IV.i.29), a cogent argument indeed in Tim's case. Tim does not know that his argument itself can be reversed, that *animal ratione est stultus* is as susceptible of proof as the opposite. He had it right earlier:

> 'Tis the easiest thing
> To prove a fool by logic; by logic
> I'll prove anything.
>
> (IV.i.35–37)

Tim thinks his logic marks him as a learned man when it actually confirms his foolhardiness.

Like all foolish characters in Middleton, he does not relate his logic to the actualities of the play world. Quomodo saw his devolutionary theory of history as fact and lost all his gains. Follywit ascribed his own desire for Sir Bounteous's estate to Gullman and embroiled himself in marriage and respectability. Lucre and Hoard failed to outwit Witgood because they failed to admit the possibility of change in a carouser and ne'er-do-well. In each case the fool confounds preconceptions of events with events themselves. The future revenges itself on those who misunderstand it, quite often by turning the fool's logic back on himself.

When Whorehound, wounded by Touchwood Junior, fears he is dying, he retreats into a strict morality that calls for him to reject absolutely the Allwits and their children. The Allwits pay him off in kind; if he is repentant sinner, they are offended burghers. When he sees Whorehound destitute, "honest" Allwit bids Sir Walter's servants leave and tells them to take "your murderer along with you." He applies Whorehound's own logic to the situation:

> *Allwit.*   I must tell you, sir,
> You have been somewhat bolder in my house

Than I could well like of; I suffer'd you
Till it stuck here at my heart; I tell you truly
I thought you had been familiar with my wife once.
(V.i.141–45)

The Yellowhammers' actuarial approach to child raising
plays into Touchwood Junior's hands. He knows that "Love
that's wise blinds parents' eyes" (I.i.190-91) and uses his
cunning to blind completely characters already myopic with
greed. The Yellowhammers are seriously hampered by their
economic frame of reference. When Moll escapes once and
is recaptured, they do not reason with her but place her
under lock and key, like a piece of property. When she
"dies" they try to recoup their loss immediately by marrying
Tim to the Welshwoman, a scheme that only gives the
Touchwoods time to spirit Moll away. Even in his final
reckoning, Yellowhammer has an eye to the bill:

So Fortune seldom deals two marriages
With one hand, and both lucky; the best is,
One feast will serve them both! Marry, for room,
I'll have the dinner kept in Goldsmiths' Hall,
To which, kind gallants, I invite you all.
(V.iv.113–17)

Sir Oliver's obsession is having children, an *idée fixe* that
Touchwood Senior can manipulate to advantage. The Kixes'
quarrels over sterility lock them into rigid positions. Sir
Oliver refuses to accept the logic of fact, that he, as an old
man, is the more likely culprit. Touchwood plays on his
delusions in giving him the potion and sending him off on
horseback to Ware, a town famous for its assignations.
While the old man is out "riding," Touchwood does for
him what he cannot do for himself.

In each case, the successful characters are able to appre-
hend the truth of the existential situation. They trust to
events and to their naked wit rather than to sterile logic.

One is as one acts; being is dependent upon action, not reputation or preconception.

The experiences of many of the characters attest that men are easily proved fools; man's descent into foolishness is a very basic comic motif. A more sophisticated pattern involves the fool's rise to wisdom, a road traveled by several of *Chaste Maid*'s characters. Some of the fools do attain a minor excellence. Maudline and Yellowhammer surprise everyone—and achieve a momentary triumph—by accepting Moll's marriage. Even Tim compensates for all his witless jests with his last remark: "And for my mountains, I'll mount upon—" (V.iv.111). The comment is one of the play's most bawdy puns; Tim's delivering it shocks and pleases, for no one expects wit from him. Even the "decayed" Touchwoods rise to predominance in the play world only after suffering a number of defeats. Whorehound treats them with contempt after their first effort to abduct Moll (III.i.48-58), but they defeat him in the end.

The man who fools Whorehound most completely is the play's chief wise fool. Allwit is a complex and contradictory figure, at once "all witty" and wittol, a complaisant cuckold. He is shrewd enough to arrange a pleasant life for himself; Whorehound keeps him as much as he does Mistress Allwit. But he must wear horns, at which every man laughs, in order to enjoy the horn of plenty. Despite this handicap, he moves easily and serenely through the play, quite satisfied with a reasonable share of simple comfort.

What some find disturbing is the extent of the concession he makes to gain his pleasures. The wittol is subject to even greater scorn than the cuckold, who at least does not realize and assent to his failure in one of the most basic human relationships. The complaisant cuckold wallows in his own degradation. Thus Allwit and his attitude account for much of the squeamishness the play has evoked; if, as some suggest, the play exhibits a "disturbing vitality" and "pervasive squalor," it is Allwit who is disturbing and squalid.[14]

14. Schoenbaum, *"Chaste Maid,"* p. 298.

But Allwit has not been sufficiently understood. He is a quite conventional creation. The notion of exultant wittolry is humorous precisely because Allwit is so literary. Middleton works a change here on the figure of the stage cuckold, who ordinarily is almost phobic about his situation.[15] The comedy stems from Allwit's acting in a way exactly opposed to what is expected of him.

In a world where *succubae* can converse with men, where inexperienced young men are frightfully clever, where people exchange disguise for disguise with bewildering rapidity, Allwit's actions seem almost plausible. We partially assent to his reasoning as he describes Whorehound's worries and his own ease:

> I see these things, but like a happy man
> I pay for none at all; yet fools think's mine;
> I have the name, and in his gold I shine;
> And where some merchants would in soul kiss hell
> To buy a paradise for their wives, and dye
> Their conscience in the bloods of prodigal heirs
> To deck their night-piece, yet all this being done,
> Eaten with jealousy to the inmost bone,—
> As what affliction nature more constrains
> Than feed the wife plump for another's veins?—
> These torments stand I free of; I am as clear
> From jealousy of a wife as from the charge:
> O, two miraculous blessings! 'Tis the knight
> Hath took that labour all out of my hands:
> I may sit still and play; he's jealous for me,
> Watches her steps, sets spies; I live at ease,
> He has both the cost and torment: when the strings
> Of his heart frets, I feed, laugh, or sing. . . .
>
> (I.ii.38–55)

What he says has an element of truth: jealousy is stupid; raising a family can be labor; the petty details of housekeeping are a bore. He shows us how we can avoid these difficulties, his remedy humorous if grotesque. But his in-

---

15. See, for example, the reaction of the old Duke in *The Revenger's Tragedy* to news of his cuckolding, III.iv; or of Duke Pietro in *The Malcontent,* I.iii.

genious prescription for domestic tranquillity does not avoid oblique moral commentary. Allwit shows that it is necessary to take on a huge load of humiliation to get rid of petty worries; we may judge, ourselves, whether it is wise to squash mice with mountains. The reader who recognizes this laughs with as well as at Allwit, enjoying in play what he knows is impossible in actuality. Instead of presenting a brief for wittolry, Allwit provides a commentary on the venality of the petty concerns that accompany marriage. He embodies every man's wish to escape the unholy bonds of matrimony yet still enjoy its comforts. His outlandishness makes the very thought possible; his literary roots and exaggerated complacency lessen immediacy enough so that he does not evoke the disgust a real wittol might. But the same exaggeration indicates that the situation is intolerable in real life. Only vicariously can one experience the pleasures of being "kept" without conscience and social responsibility taking toll. So the play's most foolish character makes in action a very positive comment on values outside the play. Within the play world he does very well, despite the laughter of his servants and the scorn of his acquaintances; Allwit is the only character who suffers no reversals at all.

The activities of the successful in comedy are sanctioned by their very success. Allwit's life style is even more humorous because he gets away with what would inevitably bring retribution in real life. But the successful characters are not always, like Allwit, "witty rather than good."[16] As usual, Middleton celebrates a body of values—honesty, mutual respect, loyalty, an ability to act forcefully and skilfully —that allow man to make his way through a chaotic universe. Though we see little of her, Moll has a charming personality; Touchwood Junior is also basically a sympathetic character. The tricks they employ to foil her parents are more than justified by the situation.

Characters step outside the boundaries of propriety and

16. Parker ed., p. xvi.

morality but do so because the real advantages to be gained outweigh the hypothetical benefits of maintaining sterile order. Here almost all actions have as object the good of the basic social unit, the family. Even the Yellowhammers, misguided as they are, try to provide for their children. Whorehound, the only character who weakens family bonds, interferes with love matches, and stands in the way of inheritances, is also the only one expelled.

As we have seen, a comedy can be judged by the characters it chooses to do without. Dol and Subtle flee in *The Alchemist*, while Jeremy stays behind; we feel that the comic world has been chastened but not completely purified. Jeremy is a rogue but will not engage in schemes too bizarre with his partners gone and his master back. Jonson seems to give tacit approval to mischief that promotes social stability, as is signified by Lovewit's opportunistic wedding of Dame Pliant. By contrast, pure chaos, as purveyed by Dol and Subtle, is objectionable. Here, Whorehound's activities are unacceptable because he acts only for himself. That the Allwits profit by his presence does not concern him, and he consciously tries to cheat Yellowhammer on all fronts.

The play advances a morality of deeds; it rejects Whorehound's verbal piety. He continues the chain of hypermoral versifiers who mix crude piety with immoral actions:

> O, how my offences wrestle with my repentance!
> It hath scarce breath;
> Still my adulterous guilt hovers aloft,
> And with her black wings beats down all my prayers
> Ere they be halfway up. What's he knows now
> How long I have to live? O, what comes then?
> My taste grows bitter; the round world all gall now;
> Her pleasing pleasures now hath poisn'd me,
> Which I exchang'd my soul for:
> Make way a hundred sighs at once for me!
> (V.i.72–81)

This last selfish mood of Whorehound's is consistent with

his earlier actions. His sudden morality is quite shallow; only fear of death causes him to reject the Allwits and repent. When arrest becomes a more immediate danger than his wound, he tries to rush back into their arms (V.i. 109-25).

The nature of *Chaste Maid*'s tone has been a matter of debate. Such matters as the rejection of Whorehound have prompted some to call the play misanthropic. For them the play's world is a very dark one indeed, its characters completely lacking in moral and religious conviction and in normal human love.[17] This opinion seems a bit extreme. It is beyond debate that the Kixes love each other, that Moll and Touchwood Junior are a devoted couple, that the Touchwood brothers help each other at every opportunity. However, it is understandable that one might take such a position. *Chaste Maid* is a darker comedy than *A Trick*, for example. The stakes are higher. Live babies are bandied about; the integrity of families is threatened. There is a duel and the threat of death. The play is heavily physical, with its constant emphasis on the elemental and bawdy in its jokes.

Of course, the Jacobean comic sensibility was less delicate than our own. Scenes in this play would hardly elicit shock from people who thought bear-baiting and executions fine sport. Situations like the gossips bepissing themselves in the christening scene (III.ii.184-86) appealed even to such moral writers as Dekker.[18] But we must admit that there is more rapacity, greed, and hardship here than in Middleton's

---

17. See, for example, Gibbons, p. 167.
18. Dekker used the same coarse motif himself:

At the length, drunken healths reeled up and downe the table, and then it would have made a Phisition himself sicke, but to have looked upon the waters that came from them.

See *The Bellman of London*, in *Non-Dramatic Works*, ed. Alexander B. Grosart (London, 1885-86), 3:87.

other mature comedies. Perhaps the playwright is working toward the dark vision that elicited such stark tragedies as *Women, Beware Women* and *The Changeling*. But at this point of his career, several years before the tragedies, he was still able to forge a thoroughly honest statement that accepted life.

The barriers thrown up against them here are high and the stakes costly, but Middleton's characters work hard to achieve their goals, to live their lives comfortably and securely. It takes not one trick but three for the Touchwoods to fool the old ones, but they persevere and win through. The play takes on such fullness on every level. We are treated to local reference, a bit of satire, several traditional vignettes, intrigue, melodrama, slapstick, sentimental and bawdy love songs, pageantry, oceans of irony, and Tim's pedantry. Even the very minor characters, like the Cambridge porter and the Country Wench, have life and vigor. Sir Walter's servant, Davy, shows himself a minor schemer (III.ii.201-6) and a knave whose witty repartee can "bite plaguily" (I.i.109). Major characters like Allwit, Lady Kix, and Yellowhammer modulate their moods and attitudes with great versatility. Middleton presents not a cast of flat characters but a little world peopled with ambitions and desires. The play constitutes a crowded yet spacious celebration of life.

Filled with so much vitality, *Chaste Maid* stretches but does not break Middleton's usual dramatic patterns. The drives toward a more efficient, stable society are more apparent than before; more young men than ever strive to possess women and possessions kept from them by older men. Kix and Yellowhammer represent the characteristic resistance to the aging process, fight their holding action, and eventually fail. The play castigates inflexible moral attitudes by implication and explicitly punishes those holding them. It develops motifs such as the young pedant's progress, only touched on before. It works out the logic of the complaisant cuckold, foreshadowed in the earliest City Comedy, *The Family*.

All is mixed together with consummate skill. *Chaste Maid* is Middleton's comic masterpiece, his fullest statement on life's ability to overcome all obstacles, to survive and even grow.

7

Conclusion

CHASTE Maid was Middleton's last City Comedy. The few comedies he wrote in the latter part of his career were pallid exercises in the Fletcherian manner; the playwright's main energies were directed elsewhere. This seems a good point, then, for bringing this study to a close.

It is presumptuous, I suppose, to say what Middletonian comedy is not. Like the studies with which it has had differences, this study has been guided by a distinct and individual set of ruling assumptions. But the perils of applying a single critical viewpoint to works of art aside, I hope that this work indicates that Middleton was not wholly or even predominantly satiric, realistic, or didactic; that interpretations of his work that hew to the lines of particular theories of economic organization can be limited.

To turn to what the plays are: the themes of Middletonian comedy are clear from the readings of the plays. Middleton's most successful comedies follow one basic strategy: the disadvantaged labor to become advantaged. Those who start the plays at the bottom of the social scale are usually young—as we might expect—and they regard their plight with all the insouciance and nonchalance of youth. Since they have nothing and risk nothing in their efforts to escape the confines of poverty, they are particularly bold in their scheming. Their lowly starting point is at least partially their own fault. Middleton's young, generally less-than-complete innocents, have suffered loss, usually before the play begins, usually as a result of their own stupidity, cupidity, or inclination to debauchery. Their plots and schemes seek to expiate guilt as well as to seek revenge.

Vengeance is wreaked on their opponents, the older characters who have taken advantage of their youth in order to lay hold of their land and money. The young are treated more kindly, generally, than these grasping, selfish, rapacious cynics who are, nevertheless, seldom completely evil. The old often relent at the end and either admit their villainy or assist the young in their inauguration into adult society, or both. We are inclined to forgive the older people anyway, because of their high good humor, their ability at trickery, the sheer joy they take in their machinations.

The basic movement of Middletonian comedy is prior to social combat. Rich and poor, merchant and landowner, all engage in the same shady practices, take the same pleasure in chicanery. We do not see the *bourgeoisie* at the throat of the aristocracy, but rather one large, heterogeneous group containing a variety of types and characters who seem interested in the same things—money, land, wives, respectability, and a certain measure of security. The struggle of Middleton's stage comedy is the traditional conflict between establishment and uncertainty, between fresh and stale, between conservation and innovation. It is a mark of Middleton's gaiety and spontaneity that the young usually triumph, even if their victories are occasionally qualified.

The young are successful because they are possessed of a clear and lively vision. They can see that the systems confronting them are shot through with corruption, rigidity, stupidity, and selfishness. They are witty enough to realize that the old who have created and now control these systems partake of that corruption and can be manipulated by means of it. They also know, or learn, that it would be folly for them to engage in such activities for long—folly larger, less gay and carefree than their own.

The role of wit, then, is highly important. Those who possess it succeed; those without it fail. This product of intellect is one of the few signs of the triumph of the spirit in Middleton's largely materialistic universe. It is not by accident that the young are more intelligent than the old. Middleton, dealing with more than the methods of the youth-age struggle, sees into the very nature of the maturation process. In Lucre, Quomodo, Progress, and the rest we see the almost unavoidable vices of the aged. These experienced, essentially conservative operators rely on precedent. For years certain actions have brought them a certain return, and they wait for that return in the plays with disastrous result. Hampered by their self-confidence and egocentricity, they are unable to anticipate new modes of thought and action and can not see value in the new order when it finally confronts them. And it is youth's very nature, almost its mission, to confront age in just that way. Middleton has caught here one of the constant paradoxes of human development, the effort of life to move into its own future while hanging onto the past.

For the present, Middleton's stage is populated by a large and varied cast of characters, all seeking to lead lives of their own choosing. Characters from all age groups and from as many walks of life as Middleton treats desire accommodation with society, with the conditions of life in their time and place. That time and place are at first confused: those least able to appreciate land and use wealth control both; women in the prime of life are married to impotent old men; the law has little relation to justice;

morality exists only in the mouths of the hypocritical. The
characters wonder at the very ubiquity of greed and selfishness. They yearn, though in a lighthearted way, for the
return of that simpler past that—we suspect—never existed.
Within this chaotic world they make the best of a difficult
situation. They fool and are fooled, seek a modicum of
comfort and administer a bit of pain, and help those who
deserve their assistance.

Middleton's world saves itself, for sense does come out
of disorder. The precision with which action matches action,
appropriate fate meets particular vice, bears witness to the
essential economy of things. The exactitude, of course, contributes to the humor. Actual punishments of real crimes
are hardly ever so appropriate; villains seldom get their
comeuppances so punctually. But then, villainy and con-
nivance are not quite so ubiquitous off stage as they are on
it, even in our fallen times. Middleton shows us life at a
heightened pace and in quantities we could not absorb in
real life. This comic technique at once attests to life's vitality
and comments on the absurdity of man's feverish attempts
at evil. The intensity of the action renders the characters'
pursuits even more tawdry and silly than they would be in
actuality.

Middleton's comedy demands an ending in which the
successful are rewarded and the foolish punished, because
comedy hopes for a better life for its participants and for
mankind in general. But it is not a *paean* to simple success;
throughout Middleton's mature comedies those who are
successful also show regard for others, a willingness to cooperate with those with whom they must interact. The
ideal for Middleton seems to be a world in which the participants are engaged in a constant process of give and take.
They are able to say "enough"; they do not encroach on
the prerogatives of others but use only as much of the
world's goods as is necessary for a comfortable but not
luxurious existence.

The plays present, then, a positive vision of a society populated by characters who are quite human and delightful, despite the fact that they are well-worn types. Follywit, Witgood, the Touchwoods—even Quomodo and Sir Bounteous—trot their paces with consummate skill. It is fun to see how good at trickery they—and Middleton—are. Middleton's achievement stems in part from his ability to make such scoundrels, as we might call them in real life, so enjoyable. Although we realize that we have seen Middleton and others use the same motifs countless times before, we feel that there is something new and individual about these presentations of commonplace, traditional subjects, and even about the evocation of a larger theme: society's ability to renew itself gradually, naturally, generation by generation.

Unhindered by conventional moral notions, Middleton's characters still seem to turn out satisfactorily. These plays mirror the universal hope that the world the characters move into after the final curtain will be the better world to which we eternally aspire. Their revels ended, the rogues, courtesans, and miserly old men hope to inhabit the staid but pleasant and peaceable world of simple honesty and virtue that is at once so commonplace and so unattainable. They are not quite sure it will be obtained.

This vision did not spring full blown from Middleton's pen. He moved from a satiric confrontation with society to an ironic comprehension of it. His aggressive and satiric tendencies are sometimes apparent outside the satiric plays, but the mature plays do show a progression—from *Michaelmas Term* to *A Trick* to *Mad World* to *Chaste Maid*—an ever-increasing fascination with the complexities of experience. This complexity reveals itself in increasingly complicated patterns of action, formed by webs of tangled motivation, sympathy, and rationale. Concomitant with the growing complexity is an increasing acceptance of what it means to be human, a delight in good, and a tolerance for the inevitable follies of man's actions in a changing social setting. As Middleton's acceptance grows, so does the dream, the hope for renewal that the final scenes of his comedies represent.

In all this consists a new way to view Middleton's comedy. Seen in this light, Middleton has little of the color of a misanthropic sociologist or of an economic historian serving as publicist for a specific social class. Middleton was primarily a skilled artist who could write with a great deal of care and humor about characters and situations from a wide spectrum of society, characters whom he increasingly understood and accepted most positively. In employing the literary forms and social themes suggested by his own time and background he created literary works that embody, though at a remove, the complex, humorous, contradictory, but essentially valuable tendencies of the human spirit.

Appendix

We know relatively little about the life of Thomas Middleton. He was born the son of a bricklayer, April 18, 1580, in London. His childhood was apparently filled with the kind of family quarrels he was later to deal with in his plays. He entered Queen's College, Oxford, in April 1598; we do not know whether he took a degree. It seems that he did not, for evidence indicates that he was involved with the "players" in the last few months in which he should have been in residence at college. In any event, he was mentioned in Henslowe's *Diary* for the first time in 1602. By this time he had already authored some miscellaneous nondramatic works. His *The Wisdom of Solomon Paraphrased,* a verbose and universally scorned restatement of Ecclesiastes, was published in 1597. *Micro-Cynicon, Six Snarling Satires* followed in 1599, and *The Ghost of Lucrece* in 1600. In 1604 two more nondramatic works appeared, *Father Hubbard's Tale,* and a prose pamphlet in the coney-catching style, *The Black Book.*

Between 1600 and 1613 Middleton's chief activity seems to have been playwriting. He was clearly accepted as one of the chief writers for the children's companies by 1605. The plays that have been the subject of this study constitute the bulk of his work during this time. Their chronology is dealt with below. After *Chaste Maid* Middleton did not devote his main energies to comedy. He designed masques and pageants for the City, held the post of City Chronologer (in which he was succeeded by Jonson), and wrote some moderately successful plays and his two great tragedies, *Women, Beware Women* (1621) and *The Changeling* (1622). His last significant play was the controversial *A Game at Chess*, produced in 1624, three years before his death.

Quite obviously, the arrangement I have given the plays suggests a course of development. I offer little proof in the book that my grouping of the plays is better than any other and will set forth none here. The question of Middleton's chronology is a vexed one. It has been up in the air for many years and shows little sign of coming down to earth. We will need a great deal more information before we can order Middleton's plays with much assurance. I had neither the time nor the enthusiasm to attempt to penetrate mysteries that have resisted solution for generations. Middleton studies need not be held back completely by the lack of a fixed canon. Later does not always mean better; saying that *Pericles* was written after *King Lear* tells us little in itself about relative value, or even about authorial development. I have tried to avoid assuming a set chronology and generally eschewed the use of temporal comparisons. Except where dates are known, "after" and "earlier" usually refer in this book to arrangement in the text rather than order in time. My argument does not require certitude in dating the plays. The fact of Middleton's fluctuating expertise and sympathy for his creations is related to but not wholly dependent upon time.

Nevertheless, it seems wise to offer readers some information on chronology. It might be interesting to measure the considered judgment of some chronologers against my arrangement—one based on my readings of the comedies and, admittedly, on intuition.

	Chambers[1]	Bald[2]	Barker[3]	Harbage[4]	George[5]	Others
The Family	1604–07 (?)	1602	1602	1602	1603 (?)	
The Phoenix	1603–04	1602	1603–04	1604	1603 (?)	
Your Five Gallants	1607	1605	1604–06 (?)	1605	1604 (?)	
Michaelmas Term	1606 (?)	1604	1604–06	1606	1605 (?)	
A Trick	1604–06 (?)	c. 1606	1604–06	1605	1607 (?)	
Mad World	1604–06 (?)	1604	1604–06	1606	1606 (?)	After July, 1605[6]
Chaste Maid	1611	1613	Not earlier than 1611	1611	1613 (?)	March–August, 1613[7]

1. Edmund K. Chambers, *The Elizabethan Stage* (Oxford, 1923), 3: 439–41.

2. R. C. Bald, "The Chronology of Middleton's Plays," *MLR* 32 (1937) : 33–43.

3. Barker, pp. 159–77.

4. Alfred Harbage, *Annals of English Drama*, revised by S. Schoenbaum (London, 1964), pp. 82–99.

5. George, pp. 18–19. Those wishing a full statement of George's arguments should consult his *A Critical Study of Thomas Middleton's Borrowings and of His Imitations of Other Authors in His Prose, Poetry, and Dramatic Works*, Ph.D. dissertation, University of London, 1966.

6. Henning, p. x; see also Charles Hallett, "*Volpone* as the Source of the Sickroom Scheme in Middleton's *Mad World*," *N. & Q.*, n.s. 18 (1971) :24–25.

7. Parker, ed., *Chaste Maid*, p. xxviii; see also pp. xxix–xxxv.

Bibliography

Aristophanes. *Plays.* Translated by Benjamin Bickley Rogers. 3 vols. The Loeb Classical Library. New York: Putnam, 1924.

Aristotle. *The Poetics.* Edited and translated by Ingram Bywater. Oxford: Clarendon, 1909.

Ashley, William. *Economic Organisation of England.* 3rd ed. London: Longmans, Green, 1949.

Bald, R. C. "Middleton's Civic Employments." *MP* 31 (1933): 65–78.

———. "The Chronology of Thomas Middleton's Plays." *MLR* 32 (1937): 33–43.

———. "The Sources of Middleton's City Comedies." *JEGP* 33 (1934): 373–87.

Barber, Cesar Lombardi. *Shakespeare's Festive Comedy: A Study of Dramatic Form and Its Relation to Social Custom.* Princeton, N. J.: Princeton University Press, 1959.

Barker, Richard Hindry. *Thomas Middleton.* New York: Columbia University Press, 1958.

Baskerville, Geoffrey. *English Monks and the Suppression of the Monasteries.* New Haven: Yale University Press, 1937.

Becker, George J., ed. *Documents of Modern Literary Realism.* Princeton, N. J.: Princeton University Press, 1963.

Bentley, Eric. *The Life of the Drama.* New York: Atheneum, 1964.

173

Bergson, Henri. "Laughter." *Comedy*. Edited by Wylie Sypher. Garden City, N. Y.: Doubleday, 1956.

Bindoff, S. T. *Tudor England*. London: Penguin Books, 1950.

Bodkin, Maud. *Archetypal Patterns in Poetry: Psychological Studies of Imagination*. London: Oxford University Press, 1951.

Bradbrook, Muriel C. *The Growth and Structure of Elizabethan Comedy*. London: Chatto and Windus, 1955.

Bradford, Gamaliel. "The Women of Middleton and Webster." *Sewanee Review* 29 (1921):14–29.

Brustein, Robert S. *Italianate Court Satire and the Plays of John Marston*. Columbia University Ph.D. dissertation, 1957.

Buckingham, Elizabeth Lee. "Campion's 'Art of English Poesie' and Middleton's *Chaste Maid in Cheapside*." *PMLA* 43 (1928): 784–92.

Bullock, Helene B. "Thomas Middleton and the Fashion in Play-making." *PMLA* 42 (1927):766–76.

Bullough, Geoffrey. "*The Game at Chesse:* How It Struck a Contemporary." *MLR* 49 (1954):156–63.

Campbell, Oscar James. *Comicall Satyre and Shakespeare's Troilus and Cressida*. 1st ed., 1938; reprinted San Marino, Cal.: The Huntington Library, 1968.

Caputi, Anthony. *John Marston, Satirist*. Ithaca, N. Y.: Cornell University Press, 1961.

Cazamian, Louis. *The Development of English Humor*. 1st ed., 1930; reprinted Durham, N. C.: Duke University Press, 1952.

Chambers, Edmund K. *The Elizabethan Stage*. 4 vols. Oxford: Clarendon, 1923.

Chatterji, Ruby. "Theme, Imagery, and Unity in *A Chaste Maid in Cheapside*." *Renaissance Drama* 8. Edited by S. Schoenbaum. Evanston, Ill.: Northwestern University Press, 1965. Pp. 105–26.

Christian, Mildred Gaylor. "Middleton's Acquaintance with the *Merrie Conceited Jests of George Peele*." *PMLA* 50 (1935): 753–60.

———. *Non-Dramatic Sources for the Rogues in Middleton's Plays*. University of Chicago Ph.D. dissertation, 1932.

Cornford, Francis. *The Origins of Attic Comedy*. Edited by Theodore H. Gaster. Garden City, N. Y.: Doubleday, 1961.

Cunningham, W. *The Growth of English Industry and Commerce*.

Early and Middle Ages, Vol. I; Modern Times, Vol. II, Part
I. Cambridge: Cambridge University Press, 1910, 1912.

Dekker, Thomas. *Dramatic Works.* Edited by Fredson Bowers. 4
vols. Cambridge: Cambridge University Press, 1953–61.

————. *Non-Dramatic Works.* Edited by Alexander B. Grosart.
5 vols. London: The Huth Library, 1885–86.

Dessen, Alan C. "Middleton's *The Phoenix* and the Allegorical Tradition." *SEL* 6 (1966):291–308.

Dodson, Daniel Boone. *Thomas Middleton's City Comedy.* Columbia University Ph.D. dissertation, 1954.

Dunkel, Wilbur D. *The Dramatic Technique of Middleton in His
Comedies of London Life.* Chicago: University of Chicago
Press, 1925.

Eccles, Mark. "Middleton's Birth and Education." *RES* 7 (1931):
431–41.

————. "Thomas Middleton, a Poett." *SP* 54 (1957):516–36.

Eliade, Mircea. *Cosmos and History: The Myth of the Eternal
Return.* New York: Harper and Row, 1959.

Eliot, T. S. *Selected Essays.* 1st ed. published as *Selected Essays,
1917–32.* 1932; reprinted New York: Harcourt, Brace, 1964.

Elliott, Robert C. *The Power of Satire: Magic, Ritual, Art.* Princeton, N. J.: Princeton University Press, 1960.

Ellis-Fermor, Una. *The Jacobean Drama.* 5th ed. London: Methuen,
1965.

Elton, Geoffrey Rudolph. *England under the Tudors.* London:
Methuen, 1955.

Empson, William. *English Pastoral Poetry.* Also published as *Some
Versions of Pastoral.* New York: Norton, 1938.

Erasmus, Desiderius. *The Praise of Folly.* Translated by Hoyt H.
Hudson. Princeton, N. J.: Princeton University Press, 1941.

Farnham, Willard. "Medieval Comic Spirit in the English Renaissance." *Joseph Quincy Adams Memorial Studies.* Edited by
J. G. McManaway *et al.* Washington: The Folger Library,
1948. Pp. 429–37.

Fernandez, Ramon. *Molière: The Man Seen through the Plays.*
Translated by Wilson Follett. New York: Hill and Wang,
1958.

Fisher, Margery. "Notes on the Sources of Some Incidents in Middleton's London Plays." *RES* 15 (1939):284–85.

Freeburg, Victor O. *Disguise Plots in Elizabethan Drama.* New York: Columbia University Press, 1915.

Freud, Sigmund. *Jokes and Their Relation to the Unconscious.* Edited and translated by James Strachey. New York: Norton, 1963.

Frye, Northrop. *The Anatomy of Criticism: Four Essays.* Princeton, N. J.: Princeton University Press, 1957.

————. *A Natural Perspective: The Development of Shakespearean Comedy and Romance.* New York: Columbia University Press, 1965.

George, David. "Thomas Middleton's Sources: A Survey." *N. & Q.,* n.s. 18 (1971) : 17–24.

Gibbons, Brian. *Jacobean City Comedy: A Study of Satiric Plays by Jonson, Marston and Middleton.* Cambridge, Mass.: Harvard University Press, 1968.

Gombrich, E. H. *Art and Illusion: A Study in the Psychology of Pictorial Representation.* 2nd ed. Princeton, N. J.: Princeton University Press, 1961.

Gosson, Stephen. *The School of Abuse.* Edited by Edward Arber. London: Murray, 1868.

Greene, Robert. *The Life and Complete Works in Prose and Verse.* Edited by Alexander B. Grosart. 15 vols. London: The Huth Library, 1881–86.

————. *The Blacke Bookes Messenger. Cuthbert Conny-Catcher: The Defense of Conny-Catching.* Edited by G. B. Harrison. 1st eds., 1592; facsimile reprint, 1924; 2nd reprint Edinburgh: University of Edinburgh Press, 1966.

Gregg, Kate L. *Thomas Dekker: A Study in Economic and Social Backgrounds.* Seattle: University of Washington Press, 1924.

Hall, Joseph. *Virgidemiarum: Satires in Six Books.* Oxford: R. Clements, 1753.

Hallett, Charles. "*Volpone* as the Source of the Sickroom Scheme in Middleton's *Mad World.*" *N. & Q.,* n.s. 18 (1971):24–25.

Harbage, Alfred. *Annals of English Drama: 975–1700.* Revised by S. Schoenbaum. London: Methuen, 1964.

————. *Shakespeare and the Rival Traditions.* New York: Macmillan, 1952.

————. *Shakespeare's Audience.* New York: Columbia University Press, 1941.

Hazlitt, William Carew, ed. *Shakespeare Jest-Books: Reprints of the Early and Very Rare Jest-Books Supposed to Have Been Used by Shakespeare.* 3 vols. London: Willis & Sotheran, 1864.

Henslowe, Philip. *Diary.* Edited by W. W. Greg. 2 vols. London: A. H. Bullen, 1904–08.

Hexter, Jack H. *Reappraisals in History.* Evanston, Ill.: Northwestern University Press, 1961.

Heywood, Thomas. *An Apology for Actors.* Edited by John Payne Collier. 1st ed. 1612; reprinted London: The Shakespeare Society, 1841.

Highet, Gilbert. *Juvenal the Satirist: A Study.* Oxford: Clarendon, 1954.

Holmes, David M. *The Art of Thomas Middleton: A Critical Study.* Oxford: The Clarendon Press, 1970.

Holzknecht, Karl J. "The Dramatic Structure of *The Changeling.*" *Renaissance Papers.* Edited by Allan H. Gilbert. Columbia: University of South Carolina Press, 1954. Pp. 77–87.

Hunningher, Benjamin. *The Origin of the Theatre.* New York: Hill and Wang, 1961.

Huizinga, Johan. *Homo Ludens: A Study of the Play Element in Culture.* Boston: Beacon Press, 1955.

Jonson, Ben. *Works.* Edited by C. H. Herford, Percy and Evelyn Simpson. 11 vols. Oxford: Clarendon Press, 1925–53.

Juvenal. *Satires.* Translated by Rolfe Humphries. Bloomington: University of Indiana Press, 1958.

Kaiser, Walter J. *Praisers of Folly: Erasmus, Rabelais, Shakespeare.* Cambridge, Mass.: Harvard University Press, 1963.

Kernan, Alvin. *The Cankered Muse: Satire in the English Renaissance.* New Haven: Yale University Press, 1959.

Kirsch, Arthur C. *Jacobean Dramatic Perspectives.* Charlottesville: University Press of Virginia, 1972.

Knights, L. C. *Drama and Society in the Age of Jonson.* London: Chatto and Windus, 1937.

Langer, Susanne K. *Feeling and Form: A Theory of Art.* New York: Scribner's, 1953.

Levin, Richard. "The Dampit Scenes in *A Trick to Catch the Old One.*" *MLQ* 25 (1964): 140–52.

———. "The Family of Lust and *The Family of Love.*" *SEL* 6 (1966): 309–22.

———. "The Four Plots of *Chaste Maid in Cheapside.*" *RES* 45 (1965): 14–24.

————. *The Multiple Plot in English Renaissance Drama*. Chicago: University of Chicago Press, 1971.

————. "Name Puns in *The Family of Love*." *N. & Q.*, n.s. 12 (1965) : 340–42.

Lipking, Joanna Brizdle. *Traditions of the* Facetiae *and Their Influence in Tudor England*. Columbia University Ph.D. dissertation, 1970.

Lipson, Ephraim. *The Economic History of England*. 3rd ed. London: Black, 1943.

Lucian. *Satires*. Translated by A. M. Harmon *et al*. 8 vols. The Loeb Classical Library. New York: Macmillan, 1913.

Lukacs, George. *Studies in European Realism*. Introduction by Alfred Kazin. New York: Grosset and Dunlap, 1964.

Lynch, Kathleen M. *The Social Mode of Restoration Comedy*. University of Michigan Publications in Language and Literature. Vol. III. New York: Macmillan, 1926.

Marotti, Arthur. "Fertility and Comic Form in *A Chaste Maid in Cheapside*." *Comparative Drama* 3 (1969) : 65–74.

Marston, John. *Plays*. Edited by H. Harvey Wood. 3 vols. Edinburgh: Oliver and Boyd, 1934–38.

————. *The Dutch Courtesan*. Edited by M. L. Wine. Regents Renaissance Drama Series. Lincoln: University of Nebraska Press, 1965.

Maxwell, Baldwin. "Thomas Middleton's *Your Five Gallants*." *PQ* 30 (1951) : 30–39.

————. "Middleton's *Michaelmas Term*." *PQ* 22 (1943) : 29–35.

————. "Middleton's *The Phoenix*." *Joseph Quincy Adams Memorial Studies*. Edited by J. G. McManaway *et al*. Washington: The Folger Library, 1948. Pp. 743–53.

Middleton, Thomas. *Works*. Edited by A. H. Bullen. 8 vols. London: John C. Nimmo, 1885–86.

————. *Plays*. Edited by Havelock Ellis. Introduction by Algernon Charles Swinburne. The Mermaid Series. London: Unwin, n.d.

————. *Plays*. Edited by Martin W. Sampson. New York: American Book, 1915.

————. *A Chaste Maid in Cheapside*. Edited by R. B. Parker. The Revels Plays. London: Methuen, 1969.

————. *A Game at Chess*. Edited by J. W. Harper. The New Mermaids. London: Benn, 1966.

————. *A Mad World, My Masters.* Edited by Standish Henning. Regents Renaissance Drama Series. Lincoln: University of Nebraska Press, 1965.

————. *Michaelmas Term.* Edited by Richard Levin. Regents Renaissance Drama Series. Lincoln: University of Nebraska Press, 1966.

————. *A Trick to Catch the Old One.* Edited by Charles Barber. Fountainwell Drama Texts. Edinburgh: Oliver and Boyd, 1968.

———— and Rowley, William. *The Changeling.* Edited by N. W. Bawcutt. Cambridge, Mass.: Harvard University Press, 1958.

Moore, John Robert. "The Contemporary Significance of Middleton's *A Game at Chesse.*" *PMLA* 50 (1935):761–68.

Murray, Gilbert. *The Classical Tradition in Poetry.* Cambridge, Mass.: Harvard University Press, 1927.

Murray, J. T. *English Dramatic Companies: 1558–1642.* 2 vols. Boston: Houghton, Mifflin, 1910.

Onions, C. T., ed. *Shakespeare's England: An Account of the Life & Manners of His Age.* Oxford: Clarendon Press, 1916.

Parker, R. B. "Middleton's Experiments with Comedy and Judgement." *Jacobean Drama.* Edited by John Russell Brown and Bernard Harris. New York: St. Martin's, 1960.

Peter, John Desmond. *Complaint and Satire in Early English Literature.* Oxford: Clarendon Press, 1956.

Phialas, P. G. "Middleton's Early Contact with the Law." *SP* 52 (1955):186–94.

Plautus. *Plays.* Translated by Paul Nixon. 5 vols. The Loeb Classical Library. New York: Putnam, 1916.

Potts, L. J. *Comedy.* London: Hutchinson, 1966.

Power, William. "Middleton's Way with Names." *N. & Q.,* n.s. 7 (1960):26–29; 56–61; 95–98; 136–40; 175–79.

Ricks, Christopher. "The Moral and Poetic Structure of *The Changeling.*" *Essays in Criticism* 10 (1960):290–306.

Schelling, Felix E. *Elizabethan Drama: 1558–1642.* 2 vols. Boston: Houghton, Mifflin, 1908.

————. *Elizabethan Playwrights: A Short History of the English Drama from Medieval Times to the Closing of the Theatres in 1642.* New York: Harper, 1925.

Schoenbaum, Samuel. "*A Chaste Maid in Cheapside* and Middleton's City Comedy." *Studies in the English Renaissance Drama in*

Memory of Karl Julius Holzknecht. Edited by J. W. Bennett *et al.* New York: New York University Press, 1959.

———. *Middleton's Tragedies: A Critical Study.* New York: Columbia University Press, 1955.

———. "Middleton's Tragicomedies." *MP* 54 (1956):7–19.

———. "A New Middleton Record." *MLR* 55 (1960):82–84.

———. "The Precarious Balance of John Marston." *PMLA* 67 (1952): 1069–78.

Shakespeare, William. *The First Part of King Henry IV.* Edited by A. R. Humphreys. 6th ed. The Arden Shakespeare. London: Methuen, 1960.

Slights, William W. E. "The Trickster-Hero and Middleton's *A Mad World, My Masters.*" *Comparative Drama* 3 (1969): 87–98.

Stone, Lawrence. "The Anatomy of the Elizabethan Aristocracy." *EHR* 18 (1948):1–53.

———. *The Crisis of the Aristocracy: 1558–1641.* Oxford: Clarendon Press, 1965.

Stubbes, Philip. *Anatomye of the Abuses in England.* Edited by Frederick J. Furnivall. London: The New Shakespeare Society, 1879.

Sutherland, James Runcieman. *English Satire.* Cambridge: Cambridge University Press, 1958.

Symons, Arthur. *Studies in the Elizabethan Drama.* New York: Dutton, 1919.

Tawney, R. H. *Religion and the Rise of Capitalism: A Historical Study.* New York: Harcourt, Brace, 1926.

———. "The Rise of the Gentry, 1558–1640." *EHR* 11 (1941): 1–38.

Terence. *Plays.* Translated by John Sargeaunt. 2 vols. The Loeb Classical Library. New York: Macmillan, 1920–25.

Thomson, J. A. K. *Irony: An Historical Introduction.* London: Allen & Unwin, 1926.

Trevelyan, G. M. *English Social History: A Study of Six Centuries, Chaucer to Queen Victoria.* London: Longmans, Green, 1944.

Trevor-Roper, H. R. "The Elizabethan Aristocracy: An Anatomy Anatomized." *EHR,* 2nd ser. 3 (1950):279–98.

———. *The Gentry: 1540–1640.* The *Economic History Review* Supplements 1, n.d.

Unwin, George. *Industrial Organization in the Sixteenth and Seventeenth Centuries.* Oxford: Clarendon, 1904.

Ward, Adolphus W. *A History of English Dramatic Literature to the Death of Queen Anne.* London: Macmillan, 1899.

Weber, Max. *The Protestant Ethic and the Spirit of Capitalism.* Translated by Talcott Parsons. London: Allen & Unwin, 1930.

Welsford, Enid. *The Fool.* Garden City, N. Y.: Doubleday, 1961.

Wheeler, John. *A Treatise of Commerce.* Edited by George Burton Hotchkiss. New York: New York University Press, 1931.

Williams, Robert I. "Machiavelli's *Mandragola,* Touchwood Senior, and the Comedy of Middleton's *A Chaste Maid in Cheapside.*" *SEL* 10 (1970): 385–96.

Willson, David Harris. *King James VI and I.* New York: Oxford University Press, 1956.

Wright, Louis B. *Middle Class Culture in Elizabethan England.* 1st ed., 1935; reprinted Ithaca, N. Y.: Cornell University Press, 1958.

Index

Adulescens, 37, 49, 53, 54. *See* Youth-age conflict
Aristocracy, the, 21, 28
Aristophanes, 43, 44, 45
Attic comedy, 84

Bald, R. C., 33, 171–72
Barber, Charles, 102
Barker, R. H., 17, 82, 88n, 93n, 113, 171–72
Beaumont, Francis and John Fletcher, 137; *A King and No King,* 140; *The Maid's Tragedy,* 140
Bergson, Henri, 48–49
Bishop of London, 44
Black Book, The, 169
Bradbrook, Muriel, 17, 94
Brecht, Bertolt, 23
Bullen, A. H., 58, 88n

Calvinism, 25–26
Capitalism, 26–27, 32, 36
Chambers, E. K., 171–72
Changeling, The, 78, 123, 161, 170

Characterization, 39–40; in *Chaste Maid,* 161; in satiric plays, 77; in *A Trick,* 107–8, 114–16
Chaste Maid in Cheapside, A, 20, 37, 43, 56, 78, 105n, 167, 169, 171; appearance and reality in, 154–55; attitudes toward children in, 152–53, 155; characterization in, 161; critical opinion of, 141, 150, 156, 160; *discussed, 137–62;* ethics situational in, 150–51, 158–60; family basic unit in, 140, 142; fertility in, 145–46; love and marriage in, 142–48; moral vision of, 154–55, 158–60; multiple plot in, 138–41; paradox in, 142–62; sexual attitudes in, 142–53; *senex* in, 149–50; society in, 158–59; sources of, 36; tone of, 160–61; wisdom and folly in, 153–60; youth-age conflict in, 161
Chatterji, Ruth, 81n–82, 141n
Chaucer, Geoffrey, 35, 61, 83
City, the: in *Michaelmas Term,* 81,

183